20p

Richard Kraut is Morrison Professor of the Humanities at North... ... the State, *Aristotle on the Human Good*, *What is Good and Why*, and the editor of *The Cambridge Companion to Plato*.

G000246000

HOW TO READ

PLATO

RICHARD KRAUT

GRANTA

Granta Publications, 12 Addison Avenue, London W11 4QR

First published in Great Britain by Granta Books, 2008

A CIP catalogue record for this book
is available from the British Library.

1 3 5 7 9 10 8 6 4 2

ISBN 978 1 84708 032 5

Printed and bound in Great Britain
by CPI Bookmarque, Croydon

In memory of Jim Hilton

CONTENTS

SERIES EDITOR'S FOREWORD

How am I to read *How to Read*?

This series is based on a very simple, but novel idea. Most beginners' guides to great thinkers and writers offer either potted biographies or condensed summaries of their major works, or perhaps even both. *How to Read*, by contrast, brings the reader face-to-face with the writing itself in the company of an expert guide. Its starting point is that in order to get close to what a writer is all about, you have to get close to the words they actually use and be shown how to read those words.

Every book in the series is in a way a masterclass in reading. Each author has selected ten or so short extracts from a writer's work and looks at them in detail as a way of revealing their central ideas and thereby opening doors on to a whole world of thought. Sometimes these extracts are arranged chronologically to give a sense of a thinker's development over time, sometimes not. The books are not merely compilations of a thinker's most famous passages, their 'greatest hits', but rather they offer a series of clues or keys that will enable readers to go on and make discoveries of their own. In addition to the texts and readings, each book provides a short biographical chronology and suggestions for further reading, Internet resources, and so on. The books in the *How to Read* series don't claim to tell you all you need to know about Freud, Nietzsche and Darwin, or indeed Shakespeare and the Marquis de Sade, but they do offer the best starting point for further exploration.

Unlike the available second-hand versions of the minds that have shaped our intellectual, cultural, religious, political and scientific landscape, *How to Read* offers a refreshing set of first-hand encounters with those minds. Our hope is that these books will, by turn, instruct, intrigue, embolden, encourage and delight.

Simon Critchley
New School for Social Research, New York

INTRODUCTION

Plato's voluminous writings – they fill over 1,700 pages in the most recent edition of his collected works translated into English – are remarkable for the wide range of philosophical topics they address and the depth of the questions they raise. They ask what kind of life human beings should live; what we should take most seriously; what sorts of beings we are. They probe the nature of the universe in which we find ourselves, and ask how we can take our proper place within it. How should we organize ourselves into communities, and what sorts of laws are best for us? And they go further – questioning whether it is possible to know the answers to these questions, or whether we can only make guesses. What is it to know something? By what methods can knowledge be acquired, and what obstacles do we face as we search for it? The pursuit of these questions leads Plato to many of the fundamental problems of ethics, politics, religion, art, science, mathematics, the human mind, love and friendship, pleasure and sex – and this is only a partial list.

His written works take the form of dialogues, and although each can be studied in isolation from the others and understood in its own terms, when they are read systematically and in relation to each other, his stature as a systematic, rigorous and profound thinker of the first order becomes manifest. He is also an exploratory and tentative writer: thoughts may be proposed with some hesitancy in one dialogue and their provisional nature acknowledged, and then emerge again in another work, often in a somewhat different guise. His restless attempts to keep thinking more deeply convey the sense that his philosophy is not to be understood as a complete and finished system – and perhaps that a complete philosophy will never be, and can never be, finally achieved. He finds problematic the very idea of a philosophical system as a finished product, something one need only consult, as one would consult facts in an encyclopedia. Philosophy as he conceives it cannot rob us of our need to struggle with intellectual problems and to make them our own.

No previous thinker in the West had achieved such scope and depth, and that distinction would by itself make him a writer of the greatest importance. Yet what makes Plato a great philosopher is not simply that he wrote about so much, or that so much of his thought is still of relevance, but also the manner in which he wrote. His liveliness as an author is a result of the great artistry of many of his dialogues, coupled with the audacity of the ideas that fill his pages. He intends to unsettle his readers, and to win them over to a philosophical way of life. That is the principal reason why he still is read today: no one who reads him critically (as he wished to be read) will remain unchanged.

Plato's works are intended for any intelligent reader who is beginning to think seriously and in a systematic way about ethics, politics, religion, knowledge, and the arts. They are not meant for a specialized audience of academic philosophers (though Plato also wrote some works that fit into that category). That is why they remain, even today, ideal introductions to philosophy, or to some part of the subject. One cannot, for example, find a better philosophical discussion of knowledge than to read Plato's *Meno* or *Theaetetus*; or better discourses on love than his *Symposium* and *Phaedrus*; or a better treatment of the obligation to obey the law than his *Crito*. If one seeks a provocative discussion that systematically integrates religion, science, ethics, politics, art, and human nature, nothing ever written can match his *Republic*.

Yet some of his writings are filled with difficulty, and can be understood only if read carefully and many times. His *Parmenides*, for example, is one of the most perplexing and demanding philosophical works ever composed. It is difficult even to state what its topic is, but much of it is an exploration of the various ways in which parts may be unified into a single whole. Even in his more accessible writings, Plato does not protect his readers from intellectual challenges. His goal is to lead us from shallow to deeper waters. In his more difficult works, he expects his readers to have already cut their teeth on his other writings. Occasionally, he alerts the reader to the dependency of his dialogues on others, but often these clues are missing. Readers new to Plato usually find some guide to his writings essential.

Where should one begin? With which of his twenty-six or so dialogues? The number is an estimate, because some works traditionally attributed to Plato are not agreed by all modern scholars to be his. Questions were raised even in antiquity about whether some of the dialogues gathered together in editions of his collected works were genuine. There is no one right or best place to begin one's encounter with Plato. Nor are his writings divided into the essential and the peripheral; at any rate, if one were forced to impose that distinction on his corpus, there would be hardly anything that could justifiably be called a minor Platonic dialogue. Masterpieces, some short, some long, were his stock-in-trade.

Some, however, clearly presuppose a knowledge of his other works. These are *Timaeus*, *Critias*, *Sophist*, *Statesman* and *Laws* – all written later in his career – leaving a large number of dialogues as entry points into his thought. Many of the dialogues present themselves as fresh starts; Plato evidently wanted them to be enticing entry points to the philosophical life. Much then depends on the philosophical interests of the reader.

A beginner might also ask: what are Plato's main ideas? But you will not be reading him as he wished to be read, nor as he should be read, if you focus only on the conclusions at which the speakers in his dialogues seem to be driving. No less important are the reasons his speakers give for their conclusions; the objections to those arguments given by other speakers; and the dynamic relations among speakers, conveyed by the dramatic devices Plato often uses to bring his interlocutors to life. That Plato wrote dialogues and never featured himself in his writings as a speaker must play an important role in the way we read him. Although it is vital to ask what conclusions to draw from what his speakers say, equally important is what he accomplishes by leading his readers to those conclusions through a dialogue.

In many of Plato's works he not only challenges his readers to reflect more thoughtfully about a certain subject, he also hopes to win them over to the unorthodox conclusions sponsored by his principal interlocutors. Many – but not all: some dialogues – for example, *Euthyphro*, *Laches* and *Charmides* – arrive at no positive and explicit conclusion. Plato's principal goal in writing them was perhaps to show his readers how difficult it is to think philosophically about the topic under discussion. There are certain fundamental principles that recur in more than one or two dialogues, and that all of the speakers agree upon. There is also an interlocutor – 'Socrates' – who appears in nearly all the dialogues and who plays, in most of them, the leading role in the conversation. Socrates seems to be committed to a core group of philosophical doctrines; and those, we might say, are the principal conclusions at which Plato himself arrived, and which he seeks to teach to us, his readers.

The heart of Plato's philosophy, then, is constituted by several doctrines. The world that is revealed to us through our senses, made up by such ordinary stuff as tables, trees, the moon and stars, is not the only world there is. It is in fact an image of a deeper, changeless, divine reality that cannot be observed but can be grasped only by the mind. Tables, trees, moon and stars may correctly be called 'beautiful', but we must distinguish the beauty that we see in them, which will perish, from an imperishable and incorporeal object – namely, that which these beautiful things have in common, and which makes them beautiful. Plato calls that ideal object a 'form' or an 'idea'.

There is, then, such a thing as beauty itself, which is not to be confused with any ordinary beautiful thing that we can observe. That is the form of beauty. Not only is there beauty itself; there is also a form of oneness, rest, motion, triangle, sameness, and so on. The world of forms is large and diverse. In fact, whenever our words pick out a single property, what they are really naming is a form. The ordinary objects we speak of as 'beautiful', 'large', or 'triangular' are correctly so called because of the relationship they bear to beauty itself, largeness itself, triangularity itself. That is why Plato believes that the world of common-sense objects is, in a certain sense, a shadow world. The many things we call beautiful have a unity – something that makes it the case that they are all beautiful. That is what we must try to understand, if we are fully to appreciate what beauty is, and to take in its full value. The way we live our lives must therefore be based on an understanding of a deeper and invisible reality.

One might compare Plato with one of his contemporaries, Democritus, who came to the conclusion that the ordinary world we observe can be understood only if it is recognized as governed by a much smaller world of objects: tiny, invisible atoms, whose diverse motions, shapes, and sizes explain the features of the larger objects that affect our senses. For both of them, a deeper understanding of reality can be achieved only if we acknowledge that our senses do not on their own reveal the fundamental entities. Democritus's idea was revived in the seventeenth century and had a profound impact on our physics and chemistry, but Plato's hypothesis that there are forms is more radical than Democritus's. Forms, being incorporeal, are a fundamentally different *kind* of entity from both trees and atoms. They are unseen not because our eyes cannot detect them but by their very nature. Democritus, for all his boldness, did not propose, as Plato did, a new category of reality, more fundamental than that of physical objects: a realm of non-corporeal, and for that reason imperceptible, entities.

Plato held that if we reflect carefully about who we are, we will have to admit the existence of non-corporeal objects. We are not identical to our bodies. Rather, we use this or that part of the body – we decide to move our arms, or to keep our mouth shut – and the agent who controls the body is not another body; it is the soul. The soul, not the body, is able to understand the forms. That is what one might expect: that which acquires knowledge must in some way be suitable to the object it seeks to understand. The soul, being incorporeal, is just the kind of thing that is capable of understanding the forms.

Furthermore, he argues that the soul is not the sort of thing that can come into being or perish. It will not die when the body dies, and so we must anticipate a future life, with rewards and punishments meted out by the divine souls who oversee human existence as best they can. Since the soul never comes into existence, but always is, all of us have already had many previous lives, each lived inside a different kind of body. (The human soul can even enter the body of animals, and so the animals we see around us may once have been human beings, and we ourselves may once have occupied the bodies of animals.) At some distant time, aeons ago, we must have had an especially clear understanding of the forms, because the soul was then disembodied and therefore in the best position to get a good view of them. We all have the potential to recollect what we once learned about the forms, and we can realize this potential by becoming less attached than most people are to material possessions, physical pleasures, and such specious social attractions as power, status and wealth.

Plato insists that it is difficult to resist the allure of these worldly values because the most powerful forces of the human soul are inherently biased in their favour. But whenever reason frees itself from their force and can carry out a proper philosophical investigation of what is valuable, it is led to the conclusion that the greatest goods available to human beings are an understanding of the nature of forms and the harmonious ordering of our psychological drives, appetites and motives. That inner harmony is the only secure basis for just relations among human beings. The political community will flourish, and be a true community rather than a battle among hostile factions, only when it is governed by human beings who have attained psychological harmony and a deep understanding of what is valuable, and devote themselves to the common good of all citizens. The good of all is most fully achieved when society is governed by public-spirited people who have no love of power and riches for their own sake, and who have, through long study and training, developed a proper understanding of the form of the good.

Why did Plato write dialogues to express fundamental ideas? At one point in his *Phaedrus*, he has Socrates speak about the inherent weakness of all writing as a vehicle for the achievement of philosophical understanding. Words, Socrates tells us here, are frozen on the page: they are a mere 'image' of 'living, ensouled discourse'. When a philosophical treatise is asked questions, it cannot answer. It cannot know what assumptions its readers are making, because it cannot know their background and character; and so it will be suitable for some audiences but not others.

Plato, through Socrates, is commenting on the limitations of philosophical writing. The dialogue form serves as a constant reminder that philosophical understanding cannot be inculcated by books alone. It is spoken dialogue that is the primary vehicle for conveying and achieving insight into philosophical matters. Students of philosophy have achieved nothing worthwhile if they merely know what is written in philosophical treatises. They must make the subject their own by engaging in the give and take of philosophical argument. Written works are not entirely useless (that would be a very odd thesis for Plato to have accepted), but they are secondary in importance to living philosophy, which is an inherently social and spontaneous enterprise. An understanding of the matters discussed by philosophy is constituted by the ability to explain oneself to others – and not just to one person, but to those who occupy different points of view.

Socrates, the historical figure upon whom the interlocutor in

Plato's dialogues is based, had a profound effect not only on the content of his writings but also on the form they took. Plato thinks of him as the person who had most fully lived as a person should live: by conversing with his fellow Athenians, he sought an understanding of the deepest problems of human existence, and hoped that in doing so he might reform or perhaps even transform a corrupt and superficial society. Socrates had not written a word, and although Plato does not slavishly imitate him in that respect, he takes from Socrates the idea that spoken dialogue is an essential tool of philosophical understanding, and the dialogue form into which he casts his writings is an embodiment of that idea.

Plato's project, in nearly all his works, is to ensure that Socrates's conversational and ethical way of life will continue to win adherents. He wants us to arrive at certain conclusions (particularly his core doctrines of the existence of forms and the immateriality of the soul), but not to accept them out of deference to authority. He hopes to carry forward the Socratic mission and to convey the deep meaning of Socrates's life by engaging in a project far more long-lasting than conversation, but he also writes in a way whose very construction will serve as a reminder that spoken dialogue is the principal vehicle of philosophical understanding. He effaces himself in his writing not because he wants us to work all the harder to figure out what he believes, but because he is convinced that finding out what Plato (or anyone else) believes must never be made the essential task of philosophical thinking. To read Plato in a Platonic spirit is to treat the interpretation of Plato as a means to a further end: our own philosophical development.

His readers nonetheless cannot help being curious about the details of his life and the cultural milieu that shaped his thought, and it helps our understanding of him to be aware of the forces that influenced him. Nearly all the interlocutors of his dialogues – not merely Socrates – were real people who occupied the upper reaches of Athenian society or the larger world of the

Greek-speaking city-states. That world was the scene of intellectual and political ferment. Plato was born in 427 BC, four years after the start of the Peloponnesian War, which set Sparta, a tightly organized militaristic society, against democratic Athens. Athens was defeated in 404 BC, and five years later Socrates was tried and punished with death for the crime of impiety. Those events gave great urgency to the political and moral questions that preoccupy Plato. In his dialogues he considered from what standpoint such regimes as Sparta and Athens can be criticized, and to what goals a political community should dedicate itself, to overcome not only its external enemies but also the internal divisions that corrode it. His interlocuters discussed what sorts of beings the gods are, and how we can know the nature of true piety.

Plato was affected not only by the political currents that buffeted wartime Athens, but also by the intellectual developments that brought to his attention the questions raised by the atomism of Democritus and other speculative thinkers of his time. Plato is said to have visited a community of mathematicians in Sicily when he was near the age of forty, and some of his writings show familiarity with the methods and results of contemporary geometry and number theory. He returned to Sicily twice more in his life, in unsuccessful efforts to mould the regime of Dionysius II after the pattern set forth in the *Republic* and *Laws*.

After his first visit to Sicily, in the mid-380s BC, he established a community of scholars in Athens in a suburban grove sacred to the hero Academos, giving it the name the Academy. Here he gathered some of the leading mathematicians and philosophers of his time, including Aristotle, who left his native Stagira in 367 BC at the age of seventeen, to lead a life of research and writing in Plato's Academy. He remained there for twenty years, and departed when Plato died, in 347 BC, and the leadership of the Academy passed to Plato's nephew. The Academy remained an active research institution for three more centuries.

The most important revitalization of Plato's philosophy in the ancient world can be found in the writings of Plotinus, who was active in the third century AD. The works of Plato and Plotinus had a profound effect on such medieval philosophers as Augustine and Aquinas, and on the Renaissance humanist, Marsilio Facino. The central role Plato and Plotinus give to the form of the good is reassigned by Christian philosophers to God, but in several ways the form of the good and God are kindred entities: these are the eternal and incorporeal archetypes in whose image the rest of the world has been shaped, and from which it has emanated.

But even non-Christian or anti-Christian thinkers of the nineteenth and twentieth centuries have found an inexhaustible mine of ideas and tools for thinking in Plato's writings. Many of the problems that preoccupy his interlocutors remain our own: How can we achieve psychological harmony? How can communities be unified and well governed? What role should religion play in civic affairs? What is justice, and why should we be just? Is there any basis for thinking that some other kind of reality exists beyond the one we observe with our eyes and ears? Plato's writings do not necessarily give the best possible answers to these questions. But if he helps us arrive at our own answers, he will have achieved his principal goal as an author.

1

SOCRATES AND THE EXAMINED LIFE

Perhaps someone might say: 'But Socrates, are you not able to be silent and keep still by going to live in exile?' But this is the most difficult thing about which to persuade some of you. For if I say that this would be disobeying the god and for that reason it is impossible for me to keep still, you will not believe me, because you will take me to be using irony. If, on the other hand, I say that it is the greatest good for a human being to engage in discussion every day about virtue and those other things about which you hear me conversing and testing myself and others, for the unexamined life is not worth living for a human being, you will believe me even less. (*Apology*, 37e–38a)

Socrates is the principal speaker in almost all of Plato's dialogues, and one of Plato's goals, in many of his works, is to win adherents to the Socratic way of life. But what can we really know about the historical Socrates – the flesh-and-blood man who lived and died, rather than the character whose words appear on the pages of Plato's writings?

No philosophical work of Socrates exists, and we can be sure that this is because he wrote nothing. No ancient source attributes to him any written work or portrays him as an author. What we know of him comes entirely through authors who write about him or use him, as Plato does, as a speaker in philosophical works.

We can tell, and not only from Plato's works, that he was a prominent figure in Athens during the second half of the fifth century
BC. He was not a private person, someone whose life was lived
within the confines of a small circle of friends and acquaintances.
Several sources attest to his being a public figure, and a provocative man.

Socrates is the central figure of a comic play by Aristophanes:
Clouds (first staged in 423 BC, many years before Socrates was
tried and sentenced to death in 399 BC). Aristophanes would
have counted on his audience knowing something about
Socrates to give a context to his character in the play. Socrates is
portrayed in *Clouds* as a strange and unscrupulous figure, attractive to wealthy and immoral young people. He is full of silly,
pseudo-scientific ideas and dangerous, unethical notions. His
workplace (a sort of research laboratory) is burned down at the
end of the play, as the character who has been cheated by him
takes his revenge. However unfair Aristophanes's portrait may be
(he is as eager to satirize a certain type of individual as he is to
put Socrates into that category), it is clearly a portrait of a familiar public figure.

Plato and several other authors of the first half of the fourth
century BC wrote what Aristotle called 'Socratic discourses' –
dialogues featuring Socrates and other interlocutors. Plato's dialogues were not entirely unique: when he wrote them, he was
contributing – though not in a coordinated way – to a genre
dedicated to keeping Socrates's memory alive by portraying him
in conversation with others. The other author whose portraits of
Socrates in dialogue survive in full is an Athenian general and
historian, Xenophon. His *Memorabilia* is essential reading for
anyone curious about the historical Socrates, for although his
portrait of Socrates is similar in many ways to the one Plato
paints, there are significant differences as well.

Neither Plato's nor Xenophon's depiction of Socrates corresponds to that of Aristophanes. Because of these differences
between eyewitness accounts, determining what the real Socrates

was like, and what he said, is fraught with difficulty. Some scholars conclude that little can be known about the historical Socrates. Both Plato and Xenophon may have been distorting the truth; perhaps neither held himself to high standards of historical accuracy.

What we can be certain of is that Socrates spent much of his life investigating abstract ethical questions by challenging his conversational partners to defend their most fundamental assumptions about how they should live their lives. About that much, Plato and Xenophon are agreed, and there is no better way to account for his notoriety. Nor is there any doubt that he was brought to trial on the charge of impiety in 399 BC, found guilty, and sentenced to death. The common assumption is that Socrates took hemlock, which was the poison often used to administer the death penalty. Plato's *Apology* purports to be the speech that Socrates gave in his defence at his trial, and whether or not it is even roughly accurate, it is indispensable to the study of Plato's philosophy, because it conveys better than any of his works why Socrates affected him and others so deeply. Whether Socrates actually said to the jury, as Plato reports in the extract above, that 'the unexamined life is not worth living' – whether he used those exact words or something to the same effect – is less important for our understanding of Plato than that these words capture what Plato took to be the significance of Socrates's way of life.

According to Plato and Xenophon, the specific accusations made against Socrates by his prosecutors were that he corrupted the young and did not accept the traditional gods worshipped in Athens, but devoted himself instead to strange, new gods. We cannot be certain whether these accusations were a mere pretext to secure Socrates's downfall. Socrates was closely associated with several figures who played a prominent role in Athenian politics. One of them, Alcibiades, had betrayed Athens in its war against Sparta – the war that began in 431 BC and ended with the defeat of Athens in 404 BC, and that is the subject of Thucydides's great historical work, *Peloponnesian War*. Another, Critias, was an anti-democratic author who played a prominent role in overthrowing, for a brief period in 404 BC, the Athenian democracy and installing it its place a ruling junta of thirty (called the 'Thirty Tyrants' in antiquity). Socrates's close ties with these figures is confirmed by their appearance in some of Plato's dialogues as partners in conversations with him. It is certainly possible, then, that champions of Athenian democracy, having defeated the Thirty Tyrants, and anxious about the possibility of future coups, thought it best to rid Athens of a man who had been a prominent ally of dangerous enemies of democratic rule and a threat to the restored regime. An amnesty had been extended to anti-democratic forces, and so Socrates could not have been legally charged on this account. Bringing him to trial on the charge of impiety might therefore have been a way of bypassing the amnesty.

Nonetheless, in Plato's *Apology*, Socrates never treats the charge of impiety as a subterfuge, and spends a great deal of time portraying himself as a man who has spent his whole life in the service of 'the god'. That is, he thinks that the jury's decision about whether to convict or acquit him will turn on their judgment about whether he is truly a pious person – someone who made every effort to abide by his religious duty as he understood it. Many Athenians believed that a group of itinerant intellectual figures – often called 'sophists' – taught doctrines that undermined morality and denied the existence of the traditional civic gods. The Greek word, unlike our 'sophistry', could be used without pejorative force, and was cognate to their term for wisdom. Socrates claims in the *Apology* that he is being confused with these sophists, and he is at pains to show how different he is from them. He insists, for example, that he is not a teacher, as they claimed to be, and that he does not charge a fee, as they did. But he admits that, like the sophists, he attracts a following. That, he says, is because his lifelong practice of publicly challenging people to defend their ethical assumptions has won the admiration of young men who love to see their complacent elders bested in argument.

That Socrates was corrupting the young, that he was no different from the sophists, and that, like some of them, he had unconventional religious ideas may have been worries that Socrates's accusers and jurors took seriously. Whether or not there was a tacit political dimension to his trial, fear of religious deviance is likely to have been one of the social circumstances that led to his death. As Socrates acknowledges in several of Plato's works – including the *Apology* – a divine voice speaks directly to him; and he insists in the *Apology* that his religious duties, as he understands them, are more important than his obligations to his fellow citizens. It would not have been difficult for a juror who had heard a speech roughly similar to the one we find in Plato's *Apology* to have concluded, simply on the basis of Socrates's peculiar religious orientation, that he was a danger to the city. After all, since Socrates's conception of his religious duties makes those duties more important than his civic obligations, he might be teaching the young people he attracts that they too should follow their private understanding of what the gods wish, and ignore the democratic decisions of the Athenian assembly.

Furthermore, Socrates realizes that many of his fellow citizens do not take him at his word when he portrays himself as someone who innocently 'discusses virtue every day', and refuses to stop doing so, or to live in exile, because that 'would be disobeying the god'. They think he is speaking ironically – saying one thing but meaning another. It would be natural for his jurors to suspect that something more pernicious than Socrates admits underlay these conversations. So, Plato's *Apology* has at least some credibility as a rough account of the sorts of things Socrates said to the jury: such a speech might well have offended enough jurors to secure his conviction.

It is a safe assumption that Plato was personally acquainted with the historical Socrates and, along with several other members of his generation, took delight in hearing him 'discuss virtue every day' – so much so that when he died they devoted themselves to writing dialogues in which Socrates engages in such conversations. Plato was twenty-eight years old when Socrates died. Whether he started writing dialogues that feature Socrates before 399 BC is not known, but is assumed to be unlikely – why would anyone want to read a dialogue featuring Socrates, when the real Socrates was still alive and eager to talk? In any case, if Plato wrote the *Apology* soon after the death of Socrates, when the event was still fresh in his mind, and the rest of his dialogues post-date this work, his career as a writer spanned roughly half a century. He died in 347 BC.

We cannot know whether the historical Socrates said: 'The unexamined is life is not worth living', or whether instead those words were first formulated by Plato. They do not occur elsewhere in Plato's writings. Nonetheless, his dialogues leave no doubt about what he took them to mean. When we read such short ethical dialogues as *Euthyphro*, *Laches*, *Charmides*, *Lysis*, *Protagoras*, *Hippias Minor* and *Meno*, we find Socrates engaged in an adversarial conversational practice; he raises a difficult ethical question, often of bewildering abstractness: What is piety (*Euthyphro*)? What is courage (*Laches*)? Can virtue be taught (*Protagoras*, *Meno*)? Is someone who knowingly speaks falsely better than someone who does so unwittingly (*Hippias Minor*)? Socrates's conversational partner sometimes ventures an immediate answer, or is led by a series of further questions to propose an answer. That answer is then subjected to careful scrutiny, to see whether it fits with the interlocutor's other beliefs; and it soon emerges that it cannot be sustained, because it leads to an internal inconsistency – a contradiction among the assumptions that the interlocutor has made. Often several further answers are given, but in the end, no satisfactory solution is found. The dialogue concludes with Socrates's admission that he lacks knowledge of the topic under discussion, vitally important though it is.

The thesis that 'the unexamined life is not worth living' means that an examined life is worth living precisely because it is self-critical. It implies that something profoundly worthwhile takes place in Socratic conversations even when no satisfactory solution to the initial problem has been found. The very process of ethical inquiry is valuable even apart from its leading to a definite conclusion. Socrates's speech explains why he lived his life as he did, and the immense value of deep ethical reflection lies at the heart of that explanation. Socrates impressed on Plato, as no other person had, the importance of a philosophical engagement with the deepest problems of ethical life, and provided a model of what it is to be philosophically engaged with these problems.

Plato evidently regarded Socrates as someone who had risen above the ordinary standards of morality and religion, and who paid with his life because that sense of superiority was resented by his fellow citizens. Throughout the *Apology*, Socrates castigates his jurors for their lax moral standards: they are above all interested in living long, comfortable lives, and can think of nothing more worthwhile than wealth, or reputation, or power, and are willing to break the law, if need be, to achieve their ends. They have never really worried about whether the ends they pursue are valuable. They might consider themselves to be good people, but their virtue is a sham, he believes, if it rests on unthinking acceptance of the values that happen to be prized by their community. Each of us must find a way to assure ourselves that what we are seeking in our lives is worth all our effort. How else can we do so, Socrates asks, except by means of the kinds of conversations he regularly has? Plato is utterly convinced that Socrates is right about that, and that he was right to castigate his fellow citizens for their conventionalism, complacency and corruption.

Several of Plato's works are companion pieces to the *Apology*, in that they enlarge upon the narrative of his trial and death. In the *Euthyphro*, Socrates is about to respond to the legal accusations that have been made against him, and the man he meets in the market place – Euthyphro – is also involved in a legal action: he has just charged his father with the murder of a servant. When Euthyphro learns from Socrates that he has been charged with creating new gods, he immediately assumes that the divine voice that Socrates claims to hear is the cause of his legal troubles. The conversation he has with Socrates concerns the nature of piety. Socrates asks whether there is some distinguishing mark that makes some of our actions religiously correct, and others incorrect. It emerges that Euthyphro is unable to answer this question, and has given it no thought – and yet he is utterly convinced that he has a religious obligation to prosecute his own father.

Because Euthyphro has no general criterion or rule by which to decide what his religious obligations are, he is portrayed as a shallow and contemptible person. He may be committing a grave injustice against his father by prosecuting him, and yet he proceeds with full confidence that he has right on his side, despite his having no way to tell whether he is acting rightly or wrongly. Socrates, as he is portrayed in the *Apology*, makes that same accusation against all Athenians: they are thoughtless people because they have not examined themselves as Socrates has. It is not surprising that they will at least occasionally go badly astray and even commit the greatest crimes, while thinking of themselves as good people. Having and acting on good intentions is not enough to make one a good person, because it is compatible with a misunderstanding of what is most worthwhile. What must be added to good intentions is a Socratic examination of one's life. That alone can guarantee that the goals one pursues are genuinely valuable.

Plato is very close to saying, in the *Apology* and the *Euthyphro*, that only philosophers – people as devoted to philosophical conversation as Socrates – can be virtuous. (He will put precisely that idea into Socrates's mouth in the *Phaedo*.) We should recognize how radical a claim this is, and how masterful Plato's attempt is to lead us to accept it. It might seem to be a matter of common sense that the standards we must meet, if we are to count as good people, are not demanding. We often assume that what is morally required of us is an obvious matter – something that is written in our hearts and accessible to all people of good will. But Plato's portrait of Socrates undermines this assumption and replaces it with the very different idea that we must ask ourselves difficult philosophical questions, if we are to have something more valuable than the mere appearance of virtue.

In the *Crito*, Socrates has been sentenced to death, and is awaiting the day of his execution. A member of his circle, Crito, offers to bribe the jailers to allow Socrates to escape from prison and continue his life as an exile from Athens. After all, Crito says, Socrates is innocent of the charges against him, and is being unjustly put to death. He owes it to his friends to remain alive. The *Crito*, like the *Euthyphro*, pretends to be an account of a conversation that actually took place, but we have no way of telling whether anything resembling it occurred. Plato's goal is to round out his portrait of Socrates's moral superiority. No doubt, Socrates could have escaped from prison, had he wanted to; it is unlikely that Plato would have represented this as a possible course of events, had it not been so. But Plato claims that Socrates would not have accepted an offer to escape, because he would never violate the laws and overturn the legitimate procedures of his city, even when those laws and procedures call for his death.

What Plato is asking his readers to believe, above all, is that Socrates was the sort of person who would give up his life, disappoint his friends, and leave his children fatherless, because he was convinced that justice required him to do so. He defied the common-sense conviction (as widely shared today as it was in the ancient world) that an innocent person convicted of a crime and condemned to death may legitimately try to evade his punishment.

Plato's narration of the trial and death of Socrates comes to a close in the *Phaedo*. It purports to be the conversation Socrates had with some of his closest companions shortly before he drank the drug that caused him to die, and its subject is the nature of the soul and the possibility of its survival after death. Like the *Crito*, and unlike the *Euthyphro*, it comes to a positive conclusion: Socrates confidently gives not just one but four arguments to show that the soul cannot be destroyed, and therefore survives the deterioration of the body.

It is widely believed among scholars that these arguments for the immortality of the soul are Plato's invention, not that of the historical Socrates. Plato is not a passive mimic of the words of others, but a creative and inventive philosopher in his own right, and he uses a figure called Socrates to achieve his own philosophical goals. Born to a wealthy and politically well-connected family, Plato could easily have become a powerful figure on the stage of Athenian politics. It was Socrates who turned him around and made him see the importance of the examined life. It is our great fortune that, unlike Socrates, Plato found a way to live such a life not merely by having conversations with Socrates and others, but in the more enduring medium of philosophical prose.

2

SOPHISTS, ORATORS, AND THE GROUNDING OF SOCIAL NORMS

Protagoras: . . . everyone readily tells and teaches everyone else what is just and lawful . . . Everyone is a teacher of virtue, so far as he can be, yet no one seems to you [Socrates] to be one. You might as well look for a teacher of Greek; not a single person would seem so to you. (*Protagoras*, 327b–328a)

Callicles: I believe that the people who establish our laws are the weak and the many. They establish the laws by looking to themselves and their own advantage, and so too in their praise and blame. They are afraid of the more powerful people, the ones who are capable of having a greater share, and to prevent them from doing so they say that getting more than one's share is shameful and unjust . . . But I believe that nature itself reveals that it is just for someone who is superior and powerful to have a greater share than someone who is inferior and powerless. (*Gorgias*, 483b–d)

These dialogues are studies of contrasting philosophies, and are among the most dramatic of Plato's works. Protagoras was a contemporary of Socrates and a renowned sophist, whereas Callicles, one of the few speakers in Plato's works who may have been fictional, is an admirer of Gorgias, a celebrated teacher of rhetoric and also a contemporary of Socrates. In both dialogues, Plato uses the contrast between Socrates and these two rivals to raise one of the most fundamental questions of moral philosophy: By what standard can we test the validity of a society's rules and values? That question will be raised again in Plato's *Republic*, and there too, he uses a debate between Socrates and another intellectual (Thrasymachus, a teacher of rhetoric) to dramatize the issue.

The sophists were typically generalists: travelling from city to city, they offered training in subjects – science, mathematics, history, literary criticism, semantics, the art of persuasion – that went well beyond the elementary lessons that the sons of wealthy Greeks received from private tutors. Teachers of rhetoric were just that: oratorical accomplishment was the one skill they acquired and taught. In democratic cities like Athens, the ability to speak well before a large audience – in a courtroom or assembly – was the key to great power and so, like the sophists, these masters of the art of speaking could command large fees from the wealthy young men who were eager to rise to positions of authority.

What does Plato have against these people? Why is he so eager to draw a sharp line between them and Socrates? Plato's complaints about Protagoras, Gorgias, Callicles and other such intellectuals are specific to each of them. Nonetheless, there is a common factor that can be found in all his discussions of the sophists and the orators. They all traffic in skills that can be used for good or ill, and so the expertise they sell will do great harm unless it is combined with an understanding of the ends to which it should be put. Plato's point is that no study is worth undertaking unless it leads to a better understanding of what is good for human beings. That does not mean that we should not study mathematics and science, or acquire facility as speakers, musicians and poets. Plato believes that these are all vital accomplishments – provided they are not divorced from an understanding of value. The sophists and teachers of rhetoric go astray because they are amoral specialists. They teach this subject or that, and see no connection between the skills they impart and the most important skill of all: ethical insight.

Let us see how that critique of sophists and orators is expressed in greater detail. In a dialogue named after Protagoras, the most celebrated sophist of the fifth century BC, Socrates asks Hippocrates, a young man who is burning with a desire to become Protagoras's pupil, how he expects to benefit from taking lessons from the great master. As so often happens in Plato's works, the young man cannot give a satisfactory answer. He knows that Protagoras is described as a sophist, but he cannot say what a sophist is, or what such a person teaches, or why it is beneficial to become his student – if in fact it is beneficial. (In Plato's *Meno*, probably composed at roughly the same time as his *Protagoras*, we find the opposite, although no less mindless, attitude: a character named Anytus, who is, in the *Apology*, one of Socrates's accusers, is certain that the sophists are a pernicious influence, but admits he has never met one.) When Socrates redirects his question about the benefits of studying with a sophist to Protagoras, he replies that Hippocrates will immediately become a better man, and will keep getting better, from one day to another. 'Better in what way?' Socrates asks. Protagoras responds that all his pupils acquire the verbal and management skills needed to be good and powerful citizens.

As the conversation continues, it emerges that, according to Protagoras, a good and powerful citizen must have an assortment of conventionally admirable qualities, such as piety, courage and justice. In his view, there is nothing that unifies these virtues – and therefore nothing that would account for their being genuine virtues. Rather, they are merely the many diverse habits and thoughts that every mentally competent member of a social community acquires by absorbing its mores and norms. Protagoras assumes that nothing lies behind the moral standards of a community, nothing that would explain why these standards (rather than other norms that might have arisen) are proper or appropriate. He likens the learning of such virtues as justice and piety to the acquisition of a language. By repeated practice we become more or less adept as interpreters of the social norms that are in force at this particular time and place. That is why he says that 'everyone is a teacher of virtue, so far as he can be', and why this universal competence so easily escapes notice. Every time we morally criticize each other, or make moral demands, or give moral advice, we are invoking or interpreting the social norms that we have gradually absorbed. We do it so often and unreflectively that we do not realize that we are teaching virtue, just as we inculcate the rules of our common language every time we use them.

Protagoras is making an astute point: although some people earn a living by teaching a second language, and parents play a special role in giving their child a first language, every speaker plays at least some small role in teaching others what the norms of usage are, because those norms exist only through their constant use. The analogy he draws with moral norms is ingenious. The conclusion he wants us to draw is that although some people are more fully devoted to teaching virtue than others (and he thinks of himself as such a person), everyone who participates in a community and guides him- or herself by its rules should also be counted as a teacher of virtue.

Plato sometimes leaves unstated a crucial premise used by his interlocutors, thus inviting his readers to notice the gaps and fill them in. The analogy Protagoras draws between teaching language and teaching virtue is a case in point, for neither he nor Socrates makes explicit what will strike us as obvious, once we bring it to mind: many moral norms vary from one community to another, just as what counts as proper speech varies according to the expectations of one's listeners. But once that point is noticed, it points to an apparent difference between moral and linguistic norms: no one thinks that there is a single correct rule about whether (for example) nouns should vary in ending according to their use as subjects or objects of verbs. By contrast, we do look to other societies beyond our own and ask whether their ways of regulating behaviour might be better or worse than our own. Linguistic practices, in other words, are governed by arbitrary conventions, but it is difficult to believe that whether infanticide should be socially permitted or forbidden is also to be settled arbitrarily by convention.

Protagoras has a response to this objection, but it is not one that appears in the dialogue named after him. He was widely known to have claimed, 'Man is the measure of all things.' That too is an unspoken assumption that he relies on when he likens the teaching of virtue to the acquisition of linguistic competence. Protagoras is assuming that what determines the truth of a statement (what 'measures' it) is nothing other than the general opinion of the community of the speaker (that portion of mankind is the measure). Nothing is plain right or wrong, good or bad; rather, 'right' and 'good' are abbreviations for 'right or good according to this community'. This thesis is now often designated 'moral relativism'. It holds not only that the moral norms of different communities differ, but also that no set of norms could be right or best. What Protagoras teaches, then, is the art of speaking and acting in ways that most fully reflect the prevailing opinions and sentiments of one's community. His pupils come to him with some sense of their city's rules and values; he will sharpen that sense, just as a master of language might train a merely competent pupil for something more impressive.

Socrates does not make a frontal attack on the underlying relativism of Protagoras's self-conception. Instead, he questions Protagoras's assumption that virtue is teachable, and asks whether the virtues are a mere hodgepodge or instead form a unified whole. Socrates begins his cross-examination of Protagoras by expressing his doubts about whether virtue is teachable, but the arguments he uses to support those doubts seem extremely weak – and perhaps Plato expects his readers to recognize immediately that they are unconvincing. One of his arguments is that the Athenians, a wise people, allow all citizens to speak when political decisions are made in their assembly; no citizen is legally required to have first acquired a special expertise regarding what is right or wrong, good or bad. That tolerant attitude, Socrates says, reflects their assumption that there can be no such thing as a specialized study of right and wrong, good and bad: let everyone speak about ethical questions, the Athenians wisely say, because no one has knowledge of such matters.

It is hard to resist the thought that Socrates is speaking ironically when he says that the Athenians are a wise people, and that they are right to take virtue to be unteachable. As we already saw in our examination of the *Apology*, he realizes that other people often discount what he says, because they take his hidden meaning to differ from what he says overtly. As readers of Plato, we must always be on the lookout for signs of Socratic irony. If he says in one passage that the Athenians are a wise people, and elsewhere castigates them for their foolishness, we are justified in not taking the first passage at face value.

Another dialogue, probably written around the same time, raises more directly the question how to evaluate a community's standards, and how moral errors are to be identified and corrected. Just as the *Protagoras* is named for the most illustrious sophist of the fifth century BC, the *Gorgias* is named after one of the most successful teachers of rhetoric. Teachers of rhetoric sometimes wrote manuals on how to speak effectively, but their stock-in-trade was to teach by example. They would give exemplary speeches on selected topics, and copies of these speeches would be closely examined and imitated by their students. Summaries and portions of six of Gorgias's model speeches survive. The ability to speak well in the courtroom or in the Athenian assembly was an indispensable tool for anyone who wished to achieve prominence in political life, and teachers of rhetoric therefore held the keys to political power.

Socrates asks Gorgias about the goals of the teacher of rhetoric. Gorgias is frank: rhetoric is the master of all disciplines, because someone who knows how to persuade a crowd will appear to have expertise even when he lacks it. It is therefore his advice, not that of a genuine expert, that will sway an assembly or a law court. An excellent orator knows how to bend an audience to his will. For Gorgias, the mastery of rhetoric is the supreme accomplishment of the human mind.

Although Gorgias frankly admits that rhetorical skills help secure political power, he does not face squarely the moral ambiguity of the skill he imparts. Socrates asks whether Gorgias is complicit if a student of rhetoric uses the rhetorical skills he acquires from Gorgias to acquire tyrannical power, murder innocent citizens and plunder a city's resources. Gorgias lamely answers that he will teach his students to be just, contradicting his claim that if his students misuse the art of rhetoric, he is not to blame. Plato's dialogue suggests that if we want to explore the ethical and political issues that deeply divide people, we cannot take at face value what they are likely to say to each other. Many of us, like Gorgias, hide from each other and even from ourselves our deepest convictions about what is good and right.

When Gorgias's inadequacies are revealed, one of his students, Polus, who was the author of a treatise on the art of rhetoric, comes forward to launch a better defence of that profession. Polus is a more frank interlocutor than Gorgias. He claims that the wilful exercise of power is a great good, however unjust it may be; but he cannot bring himself to deny that treating others unjustly, however advantageous, is nonetheless shameful. When that admission leads him to contradict himself, his place is taken by Callicles – Gorgias's host during his visit to Athens. He is one of Plato's most memorable characters because of his willingness to defend shocking ideas with complete sincerity. He glorifies the murderous and rapacious acts of the tyrant: such a person, he insists, is doing precisely what nature sanctions. The rules and norms that govern all societies are, he claims, the artificial contrivances of people who lack the daring and intelligence to bend the world to their will, and who uphold conventional morality merely to protect themselves from the small number of truly superior individuals who would otherwise gain the upper hand.

If we look to animals in the wild, we see that killing and preda-
tion are the way of the world. That is natural justice: the spoils
are deserved by the superior few, who are not taken in by the
baseless conventions that unfairly prevent them from acquiring
the lion's share of power and pleasure.

In introducing Protagoras, Gorgias, Polus and Callicles, Plato
is asking his reader to undertake a profound investigation. He
does not present these dramatic figures as superficial. Protagoras
is portrayed as a formidable adversary of Socrates, and Callicles is
not as easy to defeat in argument as Gorgias and Polus were. The
ideas of Protagoras and Callicles have a powerful appeal – they
answer to something very deep in our psychology – namely, our
longing for intense pleasures, social domination, and worldly
success. Their leading ideas are subtly different: Protagoras believes
there is no way to stand outside the norms of a community to
assess their validity, whereas Callicles looks to the natural world
of animals for precisely such a standard. Readers must ask by
what standard we should evaluate the norms by which a community lives. If they can't answer this question, they may become
Protagorean relativists or Calliclean immoralists.

In the *Gorgias*, Socrates briefly suggests that we look to the
entire cosmos as a model for what he calls 'natural justice', not to
the rapacity of wild animals in their struggle for survival. The
immense canvas of the orderly universe contains a model of proportionality and limits: the elements of the cosmos abide by laws
and do not seek to dominate all other elements without limit.
The justice that is built into the nature of things is akin to the
kind of proportionality – one based on merit, equality and reci-
procity – that is exhibited by the best political communities.

The idea that the natural world is infused with moral order
and that the proper role of human beings is to play their part in
that world order, by treating each other justly and dedicating
themselves to the welfare of others, has proved to be extraordi-
narily attractive. It was more fully developed by the Stoic school,
one of the dominant philosophies of the ancient Greek and

Roman worlds. But we will see that Plato's writings also contain a different idea, which was developed by the Christian philosophers of the Middle Ages: to find a standard of value, we should look not so much to the natural cosmos, but to a transcendent and eternal order, one that is incorporeal and not located in space. We should take as our model not nature – not the animal order favoured by Callicles or even the geometric proportionality Socrates admires – and not the conventions of our social world, as Protagoras thinks, but something far more perfect. For Plato, these are the forms, all of which are organized by the form of the good.

3

THE SOUL, MATHEMATICS, AND IDEAL EXEMPLARS

Socrates: We say that there is a certain equality, not of stick to stick nor of stone to stone nor anything else of that sort, but something beyond all such things and different from them: equality itself . . . Do we experience something like this in regard to the equal sticks . . . Do they appear to us to be equal in precisely the same way as what is itself equality, or do they in any way fall short of it with respect to the way they compare to equality?

Simmias: They fall far short of it. (*Phaedo*, 74a–d)

The dialogue from which this excerpt is taken is one of the boldest works of metaphysics of western philosophy. Metaphysics is the study of the most basic categories by which we organize the world – minds and bodies, entities and their properties, causes and effects, and so on. Plato does not himself use that word, but he has Socrates argue in the *Phaedo* that the most fundamental kinds of reality are not corporeal: they are soul and form, each of them eternal and changeless. The dialogue also has a profound ethical dimension: the best kind of life is one that is devoted to the art of dying, because death is the separation of soul and body. Because the body is so inhospitable a home to who we really are – each of us is a soul – we should not fear death but welcome it. Suicide is not a permissible option (Socrates, having been legally sentenced to death, did not commit suicide); rather than taking our lives, we should live with the recognition that the pleasures of the body are inferior to those of the soul, and look forward to death as a release. The kind of person who is best able to do that is someone who entirely devotes himself to philosophy and cares nothing for such worldly goods as money, comfort and power – someone like Socrates.

Plato's reflections on such mundane objects as sticks and stones are part of an argument for the existence of non-corporeal forms. Once we recognize that equality is an ideal form, something that is beyond the equality of one stick to another, we will be open to the further idea that the soul is not some material stuff, but an entity of an entirely different order.

In the *Phaedo*, Socrates drinks the poison that has been prescribed as his legal punishment, and dies. The last page of the *Phaedo* contains a description of Socrates's death; the bulk of that dialogue is a report of the conversation he had during his final hours with a circle of admirers. The character who reports this conversation (Phaedo) notes that Plato was not present – an indication that this work is not the record of a real conversation, and that the death of Socrates is a device for the dramatization of Plato's thoughts about the soul. The question Socrates discusses is whether the soul exists after the body perishes. He is utterly confident that he will soon pass on to a better life, and he tries to convince his more sceptical conversational partners that by its very nature the soul is not something that can expire.

The *Phaedo* is quite different in philosophical character from the other works with which it forms a narrative unity. Those writings – *Euthyphro*, *Apology* and *Crito* – do not explicitly address metaphysical questions but focus exclusively on ethical and political issues: the nature of piety, the piety of Socrates's way of life, the justice of his refusing to escape from jail. In all of them, Socrates emphasizes his lack of expertise, even about matters of great ethical importance. In keeping with this modesty, he remarks, after he has been sentenced, that either death is an endless nothingness (and so no bad thing), or it is a change to another location (Hades) where one encounters and converses with all the other people who have died. He does not know which it is, but in either case, death is nothing to be feared.

In the *Phaedo*, by contrast, Socrates shows a keen interest in the nature of the soul, and argues that it is akin to such eternal and changeless objects as equality itself, or the good itself. He holds that these 'forms' are utterly different from the ordinary, perishable objects we perceive around us, and that we were acquainted with them before we were born. Although the *Phaedo* raises a question of vital and immediate practical importance – will Socrates survive his death? – its response to that question is a cosmic world view. The Socrates of the *Phaedo* divides the world into corporeal objects, about which little can be known, because our senses are full of error; the forms, knowledge of which we will be able to recapture, once the distorting lens of the body has been cast aside; and souls, imperishable and imperceptible by their nature, and therefore more akin to forms than to corporeal objects. It is not Socrates who is sceptical and inquisitive in this dialogue but his interlocutors. Even if the soul outlives the body once or twice, they suggest, it could eventually be worn out over time. Socrates, however, has no doubt. He offers argument after argument to prove that the soul cannot perish.

At one point in the dialogue, Socrates says that in his younger days he had a strong interest in the investigation of the natural world. He was eager to discover the causes of all of the things that happen 'in the sky and below the earth' – the very questions he claims in the *Apology* never to have discussed – but he became dissatisfied with his studies, and turned instead to the kind of understanding that could be achieved by means of the forms. Plato here expresses, through the mouthpiece of Socrates, his own interest, at an earlier point in his life, in questions of natural science, and his own conviction that appealing to forms gives us a better understanding of the cosmos than does any rival account. He holds that the best explanations of natural phenomena will explain why they have as much order as they do – an imperfect order, which comes close to but cannot match the perfect proportions found in geometry. He hints that the mind must play an important causal role in maintaining the orderly arrangement of the cosmos, but this suggestion is left undeveloped. In a later dialogue, the *Timaeus*, the principal speaker (for whom the dialogue is named) gives a much fuller account of how the material world derives its structure from the forms, through the mediation of a divine creator. Here Plato is giving us his own guess – he calls it a 'likely story' and nothing more – about the underlying structure of the physical cosmos. Material causes alone cannot explain our world; it is best understood as the imitation of a divine and transcendent order of forms. This hypothesis that the world is an emanation from or a product of divine intelligence has played a central role in Christian theology, and the *Timaeus* was the Platonic dialogue that had the greatest influence on medieval Europe.

Plato's philosophical concerns, then, are broader than those of the historical Socrates. He is interested in the nature of reality and seeks to understand the basic causes of all that exists. By contrast, the historical Socrates focused on the practical, ethical question of how one should live one's life. Further confirmation of this is found in Aristotle's *Metaphysics*, where he says that Socrates was not interested in the natural world but focused instead on ethical matters. Aristotle was born in 384 BC, fifteen years after Socrates died, but he spent many years in Athens among Plato's circle, and was in an excellent position to learn from others how the historical Socrates contributed to the development of Plato's thought.

The dialogues in which Socrates addresses ethical questions exclusively, insists that he lacks knowledge, and punctures the pretensions and arguments of other interlocutors are sometimes referred to as 'Socratic dialogues' and include *Charmides*, *Crito*, *Euthydemus*, *Euthyphro*, *Gorgias*, *Hippias Major*, *Hippias Minor*, *Ion*,

Laches, *Lysis* and *Protagoras*. They are often studied as a group because of their affinities. Many scholars assume that at least a large number of them were written before any of the other dialogues, and they are sometimes referred to as Plato's early dialogues. In these Socratic dialogues Plato is beginning to work out the ethical implications of what he learned from Socrates.

At a certain point in Plato's development, however, he seeks to integrate his other intellectual interests – in science, mathematics, metaphysics and epistemology – with his ethical speculations. He continued to use Socrates as his principal interlocutor (although eventually he composed many works that set him aside) because nearly all his thinking was a development of what he had learned from Socrates. But the emphasis shifts in favour of grand theorizing; undermining the ideas proposed by Socrates's interlocutors becomes at most a secondary ambition.

The *Phaedo* is Plato's first full venture into the metaphysical theorizing that would preoccupy him in later dialogues. To understand this dialogue we must be familiar with at least one of his earlier works, the *Meno*. The link between the two dialogues occurs when one of the interlocutors of the *Phaedo*, Cebes (a member of Socrates's inner circle), claims that all learning is nothing but a process of recollection, for whatever we learn in this life we also learned in a previous life, and then forgot. Learning, in other words, is always a retrieval of lost knowledge rather than a fresh start. When Cebes is asked for a restatement of the argument for this astounding epistemological thesis, he replies: 'When people are asked questions, and someone puts them well, they themselves give all the right answers, and if they did not possess knowledge and have the right explanation within them, they could not do this. Further, if someone shows them a diagram or something of the sort, that reveals most clearly that this is so.' The interrogation and diagram Cebes is referring to are presented in the *Meno*.

In the opening line of that earlier dialogue, Meno, a wealthy young man under the influence of Gorgias, asks Socrates whether virtue can be taught. Socrates replies that before that question can be answered, we must determine what virtue is. It is not enough to specify a person's conventional social roles – to say, for example, that the virtue of a man consists in managing public affairs, of a woman to manage the household, and so on. Even if these are correct prescriptions for what a good man or a good woman must do, there must be some explanation of why this is the case. Socrates insists that we ask what is the common factor shared by managing both civic and household matters that explains why these are virtuous activities. It is not enough to say that to be virtuous we must do things justly, piously and wisely. The reason we should cultivate those qualities is that each is a part of virtue – the very thing that needs to be defined. We need to know what is that whole, virtue, of which these are parts. A list of virtues does not tell us what it is for something to be a virtue.

When Meno finally realizes, after several false starts, how difficult a question Socrates is raising, he responds with equally difficult questions: how can the sort of inquiry Socrates is proposing be carried out, and even if it can be initiated, how can it succeed? If Socrates does not know what virtue is (and Socrates insists, as usual, that he has no such knowledge), then how can he begin to look for it, and if he happened to come across it, how could he recognize that he had found it? Socrates addresses that paradox (sometimes called 'the learner's paradox') by conducting an experiment which the *Phaedo* refers back to when it offers one of its arguments for the immortality of the soul.

The experiment consists in seeing how an uneducated person – one of Meno's slaves – can learn some basic mathematics. The slave, previously untutored in geometry, will, if asked the right questions, recognize that the answers that immediately come to mind are false starts, because they lead to results that are obviously false. Somehow, he already knows enough to tell when his answers cannot be sustained. Furthermore, if he perseveres, he will eventually see, without being told, how to solve the geometrical problem set before him. Socrates assumes that the slave could not make progress towards his mathematical discovery without drawing upon something within him. Since he is assured that the slave has been taught no mathematics in Meno's household, he infers that the slave's soul acquired mathematical knowledge in a previous existence, then lost that knowledge when it entered his present body, and is now recovering it, having been prompted by the right questions.

Plato is suggesting in the *Meno* that Socrates's demand for a definition of virtue, made in many of the early dialogues, can legitimately be extended beyond the realm of the practical and ethical. It is equally fruitful, in other words, to ask: What is a triangle? A square? A line? A unit? The number three? Knowledge? A sophist? A statesman?

A careful reader of the dialogue will see that Socratic inquiry is not by its very nature applicable only to questions about how to act ethically. It also applies to mathematics. And Plato seems to be suggesting that the search for Socratic definitions and the method used in the Socratic dialogues for testing them is a process that can be fruitfully extended to anything in the cosmos. We can ask, 'What is it?' about everything, although not everything will be important enough to repay such inquiry.

Central to Socratic inquiry is the assumption that hidden unities lie beneath the multiplicities we observe by means of the senses. Socrates assumes, not unreasonably, that one and the same thing accounts for the fact that justice is a virtue, and the fact that courage is a virtue, and so on. Our use of language seems to depend on there being such unity amidst diversity: when we say of two people, for example, that each is just, we take ourselves to be making the same claim about each of them. It seems natural to say that in addition to there being this person and that person, both of whom are just, there is a third thing as well: the justice that they have in common. Plato assumes that when Socrates inquires into a virtue, he is inquiring about some property or attribute – namely, the thing that all virtuous people share, and because of which they are rightly classified as just.

What sort of object is justice? In posing that question, we are not asking for the details of a proposed definition of justice, or any other concrete specification of justice. Rather, we are asking about the kind of entity that justice must be. Just as Plato wants the readers of the *Meno* to ask what makes Socratic inquiry – whether into ethics or geometry – possible, so he wants us to speculate about what sorts of objects must exist, in order for it to be the case that the multiplicities we observe by means of the senses are, somehow or other, also unified. The *Meno* does not propose an answer to that metaphysical question, but the *Phaedo* does. In the passage cited at the beginning of this chapter, it asks us to distinguish equality itself from the equal sticks and stones we see. In the *Phaedo*, Socrates insists that equality is not something that is observed by means of the senses. The senses can report that this stick appears to be equal to that, but it is something other than the body – it must be the soul – that reflects on the distinction between equality itself and equal sticks and stones.

Plato is assuming that if we study a subject like geometry in the right way – if we understand that it is about idealizations, not physical realities – we will not carefully inspect the lines and triangles that we draw in our diagrams, to see which figures are equal. One might suppose that no two physical magnitudes are ever exactly equal, because as one inspects them ever more carefully, one will always detect some difference, however minute, in their size. Some of Plato's readers might take that to be his meaning, when he writes (in the passage cited at the beginning of this chapter) that the equal sticks 'fall short' of equality. But Plato's idea is more interesting and defensible if we take him to mean that even if some sticks are exactly equal, there is nonetheless an important distinction to be drawn between those observable equal sticks and the mathematical property they briefly exhibit. When exactly equal sticks wither and rot, there still remains such a thing as the standard that objects would have to meet in order to qualify as being equal in magnitude. Those equal sticks, whatever they are made of, never themselves constitute the standard that all equal objects must meet in order to be properly classified as equal; they may meet that standard (whether anyone bothers to measure them or not), but the standard itself is not something that is perishable or observable by the senses. Equal sticks fall short of equality, then, simply because they are not themselves what equality is, and are not worthy of the same careful scrutiny that equality itself deserves. The study of geometry, properly conceived, is not devoted to taking the measurement of things like sticks and stones. That is not how we learn about what equality is.

It is not a big leap to move from geometrical inquiry to reflection on ethical issues. Can there be a perfect human being – someone, in other words, who has all of the excellences of humanity, and has them as fully as possible? Or must every human being exhibit some degree of imperfection, occasionally lapsing into injustice, or foolishness, and the like? Plato appears to be suggesting that however good a human being is, we cannot understand human goodness by looking to such flesh-and-blood models, flawless though they might be. We must instead reflect on the nature of goodness itself, and use that abstract model as the standard for our aspirations and endeavours. Perhaps there are human beings who embody all the virtues (just as there might be perfectly equal sticks). There is no doubt about their great value, but we must nonetheless realize that, in a certain way, they too fall short, just as perfectly equal sticks fall short. To judge a human being to be perfect (or, for that matter, and far more commonly, *im*perfect), we must appeal to a model of perfection. That – not an ideal human being – is what ethical reflection must be about. Plato's forms are precisely such exemplars.

4

THE WORLD OF FORMS

Visitor: . . . it's as if someone tried to divide the human race in two and did so in the way that most people here divide things up, taking on one side the Greek race as one, separate from all the rest, and on the other side all the other races . . . calling them by the single appellation 'barbarian' and expecting that, because of this single appellation, it will also be a single family. Or, again, someone might think that he was dividing number into two kinds by cutting off the number ten thousand from all the others . . . and positing a single name for all the rest . . . (*Statesman*, 262c–d)

Socrates: it would be no thankless task . . . to be able to cut up each kind along its natural joints, and to try not to break up any part, as a bad butcher might do. . . . I am myself a lover of these divisions and collections, Phaedrus . . . And if I think that someone else is capable of seeing a unity that is naturally present in the many, I follow behind him in his tracks as if he were a god. . . . I have always called those who can do this 'dialecticians'. (*Phaedrus*, 265d–266c)

Plato is the first western philosopher to have proposed that there is a realm of abstract objects and to have speculated about their nature and significance for human life. The phrase 'abstract object' does not correspond to anything in his own vocabulary,

but it is now part of the technical vocabulary of many philosophers, who use it to designate a host of entities that lack spatial
location, are not made out of the corporeal stuffs studied by the
physical sciences, and are undetectable by the senses. Numbers,
for example, are now generally regarded as abstract objects. The
number four is certainly not a concrete thing like a diamond, nor
is it a foursome of diamonds. Those four diamonds we see in the
shop window will be destroyed some day, but the number four is
unaffected by physical events.

Plato's discovery that there are such things as abstract objects
was accepted by Aristotle, who holds that in addition to such
familiar objects as this particular white thing and that particular
white thing, there is a different kind of entity, which he calls a
'universal'. This is the shade of colour – the whiteness – that the
two white things share. The individual table that is white is also
made out of some material – wood, or bronze, or stone. But the
colour white is not made out of anything, because it is not the
sort of entity that is corporeal. Similarly, the objects that Plato
calls 'forms' or 'ideas' are a completely different kind of entity
from the ordinary, enmattered and visible objects with which we
are familiar.

What Plato and Aristotle have in common is the idea that
there is a difference between the thing that has a property (the
table that is white, the sticks that are equal) and the property that
the thing has (the white of the table, the equality of the sticks).
It is only a matter of common sense that things have attributes.
So, in our inventory of what there is, we must include not only
the things that have attributes, but the attributes themselves.
Those are two different kinds of entities. Attributes by their very
nature can be shared by many things. By contrast, the particular
things that have attributes – the tables that are white and the
sticks that are equal – are not by their nature shared by other
things.

The contrast becomes more vivid if we note that when we
talk about the sun, we are referring to one particular object, the

one that is some 93 million miles from another individual object, which we call 'the earth'. But we can also use 'sun' not to name that one individual but to refer to a large group of celestial objects that are grouped together with our familiar sun because of properties that they have in common. Our sun (a single individual object located in space and made of hydrogen and other such stuff) has the property of being a sun and 'the sun' refers to that fiery object, whereas the property of being a sun is an abstract and not a concrete, fiery object. Although the sun is extremely hot, abstract objects are neither hot nor cold, because they do not belong to the physical world. Things that have some temperature or other are not the only realities. Not everything that exists is composed out of the molecules whose motion and energy give things the degree of heat they have.

Plato's discussion of forms is sometimes designated his 'theory of forms', but we should be careful not to read too much into the word 'theory'. If a theory is an elaborate, systematic, detailed body of propositions – the sort of thing we strive for in mathematics, physics, chemistry and biology (and sometimes in philosophy, literary theory and other areas of the disciplines called 'the humanities') – then it would be misleading to say that Plato has anything that remotely resembles a theory of forms. What we find in his writings is a series of loosely connected suggestions and speculations about these objects, as well as a number of problems that must be solved, if we are to make progress in our understanding of them. Plato is utterly convinced that there are some such things as he calls forms or ideas, but his dialogues show how many questions about the nature of the forms are open to further investigation. What Plato seems most certain about is what the forms are not: they are not observable by means of the senses, they do not perish or change, they did not come into existence at some point in time, they lack a spatial location, and they are not made out of any material. Moreover, they are not mere ideas in our minds, for they exist independently of any human recognition of them. That is why we should be careful not to be misled by Plato's occasional use of the word 'idea' to designate them. We apprehend them by reasoning; that is, we can get some grasp of them not by looking more and more closely at observable objects, but by the sort of reflection that mathematicians use when they give proofs about triangles, or the sort of reflection that Socrates engages in when he tries to undermine the dogmas of his interlocutors.

Plato's dialogues never decisively say which forms there are. It is obvious that Plato thinks there is a form of piety (we need only read the *Euthyphro* to see that). It is equally obvious that he thinks there are forms of equality (read the *Phaedo*), of good (*Republic*) and of beauty (*Symposium*). We could add many other forms to our list, as we make our way through the dialogues. But we would like Plato to formulate the principle that gives rise to this list. We need some way to determine what the population of the world of forms is.

In the *Phaedo*, Plato points towards an answer. Having argued that we must have known about the form of equality before our souls entered the bodies they currently occupy, Socrates notes: '. . . we know before birth . . . not only the equal, but the greater and the smaller and all such things, for our present argument is not a bit more about the equal than about the beautiful itself, the good itself, the just, the pious, and . . . all those things we stamp with the word "itself" when we ask questions and answer them'.

This tells us that there is a range of forms having to do with magnitude, and presumably Plato would add that there are many more that have to do with shape (line, triangle, square, and so on). Then there are what might be called 'forms having to do with value' – beauty, goodness, justice, piety, and so on. Looking through the dialogues, we could add other families of forms: the objects of the natural world (fire, horses), artefacts (beds, tables), social roles (philosophers, statesmen) and highly general concepts (being, sameness, change). But what unites all the items on these lists? When something is present in the universe of forms, what is it that accounts for its being present there?

Plato only gestures at an answer to that question, when he says that his idea about equality applies to 'those things we stamp with the word "itself" when we ask questions and answer them'. That should be taken as an allusion to the sort of questioning that Socrates does in such early dialogues as the *Euthyphro* (what is piety?), *Laches* (what is courage?) and *Charmides* (what is moderation?). Plato is saying that whenever a Socratic question is asked about some object of study, a distinction must be made between that object itself – the form – and the many things that share in it but are utterly different in kind from it. Thus goodness itself is a different sort of thing from the many good things that share in it.

This generalization prompts a further question: when is one justified in pursuing a Socratic inquiry? The Socratic dialogues take for granted the existence of a deeply hidden unity that underlies our use of ethical words, a unity that exists independently of us, waiting to be discovered. It is assumed, for example, that when we call an act performed on the battlefield courageous, and then apply that same word, 'courageous', to the act of a political leader, there is a single standard that these different acts meet, and that military and political accomplishments are properly classified as courageous because they measure up to that single standard. But we are in no position to know that courage is a single thing until we have discovered the underlying unity behind all courageous acts, however different they seem to be. Does that show that something is wrong with conducting a Socratic investigation of what courage is, or of what anything else is? Must we presuppose that we are investigating a unified subject of inquiry, although we have no basis for that presupposition? If Socratic inquiry is illegitimate, Plato's whole approach to philosophy fails. But it would be hasty to draw that conclusion.

The possibility must be considered that military and political courage have nothing important in common – that we really need to employ two utterly different standards when we apply the word 'courageous' to both kinds. The fact that we have a single word that is used of people who face physical danger courageously and also of people who risk their political careers courageously does not by itself guarantee that courage is one and the same thing wherever it is found. It is possible that we are in the habit of using a single word to cover two different kinds of phenomena, and that these phenomena should be called by two different names rather than artificially united together under a single rubric. The individuals who participated in the linguistic practices that led to the formation of a single word 'courage' and its application to both military and political exploits may have been unwise to bring such disparate behaviours together under the umbrella of a single term. If there can be no single account of what makes all courageous acts courageous, then there is no single attribute of courage, and no form of courage. The only way to know for certain that a unity underlies all courageous acts and explains why they are properly so classified is to propose and defend a theory about what courage is. Our proof that there really is such a thing as the property (or 'form', or 'universal') of courage would be a theory of courage that displays the unity that underlies its many diverse manifestations.

Plato seems confident that there are many, many forms, and that among them are forms that correspond to our moral terms, our mathematical terms, and so on. But if his confidence is justified, then the justification for it must consist in the success of an ongoing philosophical project that we carry out on his behalf: we must succeed in finding theories that vindicate our hunch that behind our use of moral terms, mathematical terms, and so on, there really is a unity waiting to be discovered. Plato, then, is the founder of a programme of philosophical research, rather than the author of an already complete system of thought.

In some passages, we get the impression that there is a form corresponding to every common noun, and that the existence of the form is to be taken as an explanation of the applicability of that common noun to a plurality of objects. For example, Socrates says in the *Republic*: 'we usually postulate some single form for each of the many things to which we apply the same name'. Here he is assuming that we can look to the language we speak, which reflects distinctions and unifications that have shaped the thought of many generations, as a guide to what properties there are.

But Plato also recognizes that our ordinary words are not infallible guides to reality. They are tools devised by human beings and, like any human instrument, they can be poorly designed to achieve their purposes. In the *Statesman*, a dialogue usually thought to have been written after the *Republic*, the principal interlocutor, an unnamed visitor to Athens from Elea, complains about the artificiality of the Greek word *barbaros*, translated 'barbarian' or 'foreigner'. The word *barbaros* collects together every human being who has the property of not being a Greek – a silly way to carve up reality, Plato realizes, because it treats being non-Greek as though it were a single and unified property, whereas in fact there are many important divisions among the non-Greeks. The visitor from Elea is not opposed to dividing human beings in some way or other; he does not doubt that there is something distinctive about Greeks, just as there is something distinctive about other human sub-groups. In his view, the Greek word *ethnos* (race, nation, tribe) marks out real distinctions, but there is no such thing as a *barbaros* – a non-Greek – even though there is a word that collects them together – *barbaroi*.

Our cosmopolitan outlook might lead us to complain that Plato should have had the visitor of the *Statesman* doubt the reality of all racial or national distinctions, and not merely the division of the world's population into Greeks and *barbaroi*. But we should nonetheless acknowledge that Plato understands the dangers of letting the divisions made by our words do all our thinking for us. As the stranger notes, a word that is applicable to every number other than 10,000 would not be a device that divided numbers well. The numbers other than 10,000 would have nothing in common but a name – there is, in other words, no property they share, no form in which they participate.

Plato never suggests that it would be a worthwhile project to undertake a complete inventory of all the forms there are. Creating a mere list of all the properties would not by itself be a significant accomplishment. Rather, he proposes that philosophers carry out investigations of the forms that are most important for human life – such forms as justice, beauty, goodness, love, unity and being.

Plato also recommends devising broad classificatory frameworks. His idea is that to understand any important phenomenon we should locate it on a taxonomic chart of other phenomena with which it shares some differences and similarities. Socrates insists in the *Phaedrus* that to understand what love is, one must classify it as a form of madness, and one must see how it differs from other forms of madness. There is, in other words, a single genus of madness, but several species that fall within this genus. Here and in several other dialogues (*Sophist* and *Statesman*), he often uses the word 'kinds' (*genē*) to speak of the realities that philosophy must seek to understand, and he speaks of the special skills that philosophers should bring to this project as skills of 'dialectic'. (That term conveys the idea of oral interchange with another person, best exemplified by Socratic cross-examination. The notion of opposition between conflicting viewpoints remains important even in Kant's and Hegel's use of the term.) The goal of the dialectician, as he says in the passage from the *Phaedrus* cited at the beginning of this chapter, is 'to be able to cut up each kind along its natural joints, and to try not to break up any part, as a bad butcher might do'. To do that is to see 'a unity that is also naturally present in the many'.

Forms, in other words, by their nature enter into complex relationships with each other, and cannot be understood one by one. It should be no surprise, Plato seems to be saying, that his short ethical works that investigate a single property in isolation from others come to no satisfactory conclusion. Perhaps those dialogues were meant by Plato to be teaching devices that enable us to see the limitations of asking, 'What is courage?' without at the same time asking, 'What is justice?' or raising the same question about other virtues. Alternatively, we might read those dialogues – the Socratic or early dialogues – as the avenues along which Plato first worked out for himself the limitations of a property-by-property inquiry into moral phenomena. In either case, there is a fundamental unifying assumption that guides Plato's writing in all of these works: the world comes divided into realities that exist independently of the human mind, and language gives at best an imperfect guide to what they are. Discovering the nature of the most important of these realities – justice, love, beauty – is, as the early dialogues intimate, a task of extraordinary difficulty.

Plato's thesis that there are incorporeal mind-independent realities that ground all that is valuable is one of the most influential and controversial ideas in the history of western philosophy. Aristotle partly follows in his path – he agrees that there are universals – but he argues that moral philosophy is not grounded in the existence of abstract objects. Some of the schools of philosophy that arose soon after the death of Socrates embraced a metaphysics that has room for material objects alone. The Epicureans, for example, argue that all that exists – even the soul – is made of invisible atoms. The Stoics are also materialists. Christian philosophers of course endorsed Plato's and Aristotle's anti-materialism, but some of them held that universals are mind-dependent. In the modern period, many philosophers, following Kant, have argued that only what is a product of the mind can be known. And recently some philosophers have become convinced that all the distinctions embedded in our words are arbitrary and reflect political and economic forces. They say that justice, goodness and beauty are mere social constructions, and cannot be grounded in anything but the opinions that happen to prevail. That is a contemporary form of Protagoreanism. One reason why Plato remains a part of our philosophical canon is that the issues about which he writes with such passion remain live issues for us.

5

LOVE AND BEAUTY

... Someone who has been educated about erotic matters up to this point and has beheld beautiful things in the right order and correctly is now approaching the goal of loving. Suddenly he will see something marvellous and beautiful in its nature; it is for the sake of that, Socrates, that he undertook all his earlier labours. First, it always is and neither comes to be nor passes away, neither grows nor diminishes. Second, it is not beautiful in one respect and ugly in another, nor beautiful at one time and ugly at another, nor beautiful in relation to one thing and ugly in relation to another, nor beautiful here but ugly there, as it would be if it were beautiful for some and ugly for others. Nor will the beautiful appear to him in such a way as face or hands do or anything else that partakes of body ... but it is itself by itself with itself, always unitary in form, and all the other beautiful things share in it, in such a way that when those others come to be or pass away, it does not become at all larger or smaller and is not at all affected ... What do we think it would be like ... if someone got to see the beautiful itself, unalloyed, pure, unmixed, not filled with human flesh or colours or any other great nonsense of mortality, but if he could see the divine beauty itself in its unitary form? Do you think ... it would be a poor life for a human being to look there and behold it ... and be joined with it? (Diotima, in *Symposium*, 210e–212a)

Plato's metaphysics affirms not only that there are abstract objects, but that some of them have greater importance than others. Beauty, goodness and justice are particularly pervasive in our thoughts and desires. We cannot help being attracted to beauty in the visible world, and repelled by ugliness. We constantly make decisions in terms of what is good or bad for us. The injustice of our institutions can alienate us from politics, but sometimes ignites revolutionary ambitions for a more just world. We can easily go astray and even wreak havoc if we complacently assume that our unexamined notions of beauty, goodness and justice are correct. We may have too limited a notion of which things are beautiful, good or just; or some of the things we describe with these terms may in fact be ugly, bad or wrong. Plato's metaphysics is never removed from the practical decisions we make every day. We must scrutinize these forms – beauty, goodness, justice – because misunderstanding them leads to serious errors about the way we live our lives.

Human beings, Plato assumes, are inherently predisposed to love both beauty and goodness, but not justice. People must be taught to be just to others, and will develop an appreciation of this virtue only if they recognize its beauty and goodness. So goodness and beauty take priority over justice; it must be studied in their light. Furthermore, Plato thinks the difference between goodness and beauty is small. Both must be understood in mathematical terms – proportion, harmony and balance. He has an aesthetic conception of goodness. What is good for us is very close to what is attractive, or fine, or appealing. By contrast, many philosophers in the modern period have thought of moral and aesthetic values as two distinct realms. A good person, they assume, need have no eye for beauty, and the appreciation of beauty is not a moral accomplishment. Part of the fascination of Plato's metaphysics and ethics is that it does not make these sharp distinctions. His *Symposium*, which seeks to understand our love of beauty, is full of ethical and even political implications.

The range of things that strike us as beautiful is extraordinary:

it includes songs, poetry, objects in nature, such as the stars on a clear night, physically attractive human bodies, and acts of kindness or nobility. One of the most profound ideas proposed in Plato's dialogues is that there is, in addition, an object whose beauty is utterly different in kind from the ones with which we are normally familiar: the beauty of the form of beauty.

The form of beauty is of course a property, whereas the usual things we take to be beautiful only have that property. But the passage with which this chapter begins seems to be saying more than this – namely, that the form of beauty is itself beautiful, and beautiful in a way that makes it surpass the beauty of anything else. That supremacy of beauty makes it fit to be the ultimate goal of all our aspirations and desires; beholding beauty itself should be placed at the pinnacle of our lives. That is what Diotima claims, and on any reasonable reading of Plato's *Symposium*, that is a position that he endorses and recommends to his readers.

He holds that we are right to be attracted to the genuinely beautiful things in the visible world – the sexual allure of youthful bodies no less than the beautiful symmetries of the stars and their mathematically precise paths – but that the greatest beauty belongs to something beyond space, time and corporeality. His appreciation for beauty is both worldly and unworldly, and he links the two realms together. That is why the *Symposium* has resonated with so many different kinds of audience.

The form of beauty and Diotima's conception of it lie at the heart of the *Symposium*, which is a dialogue only in a loose sense of the word, because the bulk of it consists of a series of six speeches and there is little conversation. Those speeches celebrate the god of love – Eros – and take place at a drinking party attended by Socrates and some of the leading figures of his time, including Aristophanes, the playwright who mocked him in his *Clouds*. (The Greek word *symposion* means 'drinking together'.) The culmination of the evening is the intrusion of Alcibiades, a prominent Athenian politician and general who fled to Sparta during the Peloponnesian War to escape legal charges of sacrilegious behaviour. He arrives late, drunk, and proceeds to deliver an encomium not to Eros but to Socrates, to whom he is erotically attached. His depiction of Socrates, and of their relationship, is as unforgettable a personal portrait as we can find in all the writings of antiquity.

Plato clearly indicates that although some parts of the six speeches praising Eros and the one speech praising Socrates complement each other in content, other parts contradict each other. At least some portion of what was said about Eros that evening cannot be accepted, but Plato leaves it as a task to his readers to come to their own conclusions about where the insights or distortions of each speech lie. Readers must also ask what philosophical lessons – if any – to draw from the story Alcibiades tells about his failed relationship with Socrates.

The speech of Aristophanes contains the *Symposium*'s most vivid image of the psychological power of erotic relationships. He says that long ago human beings were spherical creatures with twice the features and organs they now have: two faces (on opposite sides of the head), four arms, four legs, two sets of sexual organs, and so on. As a result of this double capacity, they had formidable strength, threatening even the gods. Zeus therefore decided to cut them in half, each human being taking on his single-faced, two-legged, unspherical form. But that led to an unintended consequence: each human being, having been severed from his natural other half, longed to be reunited with that other half. Since there were once three kinds of bodies – one with two male sexual organs, a second with two female genitalia, and a third with one of each sex – the erotic longings that we severed human beings experience fall into three categories: the love of a male for his other male half, the love of a female for her former female half, and the love of a male and female for their counterpart in the opposite sex.

Same-sex relations, according to this mythical derivation of human desire, are no less natural and no less admirable than heterosexual intercourse. There is no doubt that, like all of the speakers in this dialogue, Plato himself sees great potential value in

same-sex physical attraction. Socrates is portrayed in the early dialogues as someone who sought out beautiful young men partly
because of the allure of their young bodies. Nonetheless, Plato
disapproved of sexual intercourse between males or between
females. His principal interlocutors in the *Phaedrus* and the *Laws*
insist that it is best for same-sex lovers to refrain from intercourse.

Aristophanes adds one more element to his fantastical story of
human transformation: after Zeus cut human bodies in half and
each sought to be reunited with his or her former counterpart,
they would, when they found that other half, wrap their arms
about each other and refuse to let go. Their greatest desire was to
grow together to form, once again, a rounded whole. As a result,
having found each other, they were utterly idle, and even died of
starvation, because they could not bear to stop embracing their
lover. Zeus took pity on them, and in a second transformation,
he moved their genitals from back to front, so that each would
achieve sexual release and then be willing to turn to the daily
tasks of life. Sexual love, so construed, is a longing for the physical unification partially achieved by embraces; sexual satiation is
not its goal but a mechanism that temporarily alleviates one's
longing to embrace that single individual who is one's uniquely
satisfying partner.

Aristophanes's myth beautifully expresses a deep and abiding
feature of human psychology – namely, our longing for physical
intimacy, as expressed in our desire to touch someone we love, to
kiss, to embrace, and to engage in sexual intercourse. It of course
also expresses the idea that for each of us there is one and only
one other person who is a perfect match: this is not someone
who has certain attractive *general* qualities (for several or even
many others might have those same qualities), but rather a
unique individual – the very one to whom one was once physically attached.

Suppose, however, we ask how Aristophanes's wonderful story
can be freed of its mythical form, and expressed as a theory about
the value and nature of erotic love. He claims that we long to

find and be with one and only one individual, but he needs to specify who that unique individual is without relying on a myth about the splitting of formerly spherical human bodies. He should also say what is valuable in our longing for and sometimes achieving physical intimacy. Aristophanes seems to be saying that this desire to be with one individual is a brute psychological propensity that must be accepted as an unalterable necessity. He does not ask what value it has, and perhaps his story simply lacks the resources for answering that question. The fact that sexual intercourse often leads to children, and is the way in which one generation produces another, is, from his point of view, an accidental by-product of the current arrangement of our sexual organs. It is sexual relief that serves some worthwhile purpose – it allows us temporarily to go about our quotidian business – not sexual intercourse. Plato wants his readers to be dissatisfied with these aspects of Aristophanes's speech, and to look to Socrates for a better theory about intimacy and sexuality. Plato may also want us to ask which elements of Aristophanes's speech can be salvaged.

The speech of Aristophanes is succeeded by that of Agathon (the honoree of the symposium), and then it is Socrates's turn to praise Eros. He reports what he learned from Diotima, but before he does so, he establishes some preliminary points by cross-examining Agathon. Love, they agree, is a passionate desire for someone or for something that one lacks. Like any desire, it is directed to the future, because we do not want what we already have. If one says that one wants to be wealthy, that means either that one is not wealthy now but wants future wealth, or that one wants one's current wealth to endure into the future. So love arises from a deficiency or lack on the part of the lover: something is missing, and love is the force that makes the lover reach out to that missing thing.

This line of thought is developed more fully when Socrates announces that the rest of his discourse on love will reproduce the conversations he had with Diotima. She taught Socrates that we should not think of love as something that is directed only towards other people. We can be said to love anything that we take to be good and fervently wish to possess in the future. 'Love wants the good to be its own for ever.' In other words, there is no point in the future at which we would not love to have the things we yearn for; if possible, we would love to have these good things for all time. Someone who loves life, for example, wants to be alive for ever. Diotima then proposes that reproduction is the way in which every human being – and every animal – expresses its longing for the eternal possession of the good that it seeks. The desire to have children is a desire to replace oneself with something that will be very much like oneself; and that child will in turn someday help produce a new generation, and so on. Some psychological force is at work within us, and in other animals as well, that leads to the reproduction of what we value; we are motivated to be part of an eternal chain of things that resemble each other, all of them valuing the same sort of good thing. That is why beauty plays so great a role in our lives: we need a partner with whom we can cooperate in acts of reproduction, and it is a brute fact that we prefer partners whom we find alluring and beautiful. As Diotima puts it, someone who is in love seeks to 'give birth in beauty'.

Reproduction played only a small role in Aristophanes's account of Eros: it is the incidental by-product of the relocation of our sexual organs, and the purpose of that relocation is sexual satiation, not the production of future generations. For Diotima, sexual intercourse and, more generally, all eros, is the way living things possess the good for ever through the reproduction of the things one values. She speaks of two kinds of pregnancy. The first is the usual kind, a pregnancy of the body, which is the outcome of one's attraction to another person's physical allure, and which produces children. That is the sort of pregnancy that expresses someone's love of being alive. But there is a second and superior pregnancy: this is a fullness in the soul rather than the body, and it is the state someone is in when he seeks a partner who has beautiful psychological qualities with whom to nurture not physical children but thoughts and words of great beauty. There are notions within the lover that he must give birth to – ideas about the good things that he and his partner seek to have for themselves and others, and that they seek to bequeath to future generations. What Diotima has in mind, then, is the relationship of people who find each other alluring and beautiful because of their excellence of character, and who are concerned not only with each other but also with the perpetuation of excellence of character in other people far into the future. The contrast with Aristophanes's conception of eros is striking: for him, lovers focus exclusively on only one individual – their other half – and their love for each other serves no larger social purpose.

Diotima describes a series of steps that excellent lovers must pass through as their intellectual pregnancy leads them to explore more fully the ideas they have within them. They must learn not to over-value the beauty of any one body or person. (Note again how different this theory of love is from that of Aristophanes.) They must come to realize how many different sorts of things, other than physical bodies, can qualify as beautiful. Their ideas about what beauty is continue to grow as they recognize what is beautiful in things that are not recorded by the senses as colours and sounds are – such things as social institutions, laws, and the various branches of knowledge. At some stage, what they have learned about the various kinds of beauty will give them a comprehension of what beauty itself is: that will be the vision of beauty that is described by Diotima in the passage opening this chapter. The greatest benefit that eros gives us, if we know how to use this psychological force to serve our good, is the beholding of an object whose beauty surpasses that of every other beautiful object. For Aristophanes, eros is a force that brings bodies together and blocks out everything else. Diotima's contrasting picture is that through eros we are receptive to the whole world of attractive objects, capped by the most beautiful of all.

But cannot love also be a destructive force in human life? Neither Aristophanes nor Diotima raises this question. Their conceptions of eros, for all their differences, ignore the sick, frenzied or mad aspect of eros. Plato deals with the destructive potential of love in other dialogues – particularly in the *Phaedrus* and the *Republic*. Lovers, driven by jealousy, anger and possessiveness, can place inordinate demands on each other. They seek sexual satisfaction and intimacy even when this harms the person they find alluring. They hate those they imagine or perceive to be rivals, and circumstances can lead them to destroy the very people they love. But in the *Symposium*, the speech that reminds us of love's dark side is the one delivered by the drunk and boisterous Alcibiades, who arrives too late to listen to what anyone else has said.

Plato's contemporary readers thought of Alcibiades as an unscrupulous and dangerous man of great political and military talent and ambition. His close association with Socrates was one of the reasons why Socrates was a suspect figure in Athenian public life. His speech, given pride of place because it comes last, is one of the most remarkable components of the *Symposium*, in no small part because it testifies to the power of Socrates's personality. But it also testifies to the way erotic human relationships can be undermined by misunderstanding. Alcibiades thinks that he can use his physical allure to seduce Socrates, and he wants to seduce him because he thinks Socrates will, in gratitude, teach him how to be wise – as though Socrates was a sophist like Protagoras or an orator like Gorgias, and held the keys to acquiring great political power. As soon as Alcibiades realizes that Socrates is at the party he has just crashed and draws near to him, Plato reminds us of the violent potential of eros. He has Socrates plead with Agathon: 'See if you can protect me. . . . I cannot look at or talk to even a single attractive man without this one [Alcibiades] becoming jealous and angry. . . . He becomes abusive and just barely can keep his two hands off me. So . . . if he tries to use violence . . . protect me . . .' There is perhaps some comic exaggeration in these lines (can Socrates really believe he is about to be attacked?), but their effectiveness rests on our familiarity with the violence inherent in eros.

One of the lessons to be learned from the speech of Alcibiades is that even manipulative and power-hungry people like him have an attractive side, because they are able to recognize the moral superiority of rare individuals like Socrates and aspire, however briefly and fecklessly, to be like them. The recognition of some potential for goodness even in destructive people is part of the larger thesis of the *Symposium* that all creatures, even animals, have an inherent receptivity to what is valuable in the world. We are all attracted to beauty and look for some way of making it our own. If that innate responsiveness remains uneducated, it leads to nothing more exalted than physical reproduction, and can easily degenerate into violence and manipulation. We need to see how closely related beauty and goodness are, and we need a better understanding of what is good, if eros is to achieve its potential. To do that, we must, as Diotima says, become 'educated about erotic matters' and behold 'beautiful things in the right order' until we approach 'the goal of loving', which is the apprehension of the most beautiful thing there is – the abstract form of beauty. There is both a deep optimism and a deep pessimism that runs through this dialogue and through all Plato's works. The psychological forces that govern human beings put us in touch with what is valuable, and make it possible for us to learn more about what is beautiful and good. But love and its proper objects are difficult for us to understand, and it is rare for anyone to see all that is beautiful in the world and beyond it.

The *Symposium* portrays eros as a force that is a complex blend of selfish and altruistic elements. The speech of Aristophanes, for all its defects, illustrates that point well, because it conceives of eros as a drive that both answers to one's deepest need and brings one into unity with another person. Someone who is looking for his other half is trying to heal a wound. It is in his own interest that he be reunited with the person who will complete him. That does not mean that he wants to use that other person for his own selfish purposes. He simply wants to spend his life with that other person, and to be as one with him or her. The object of his love returns his affection in the same way. Each is constantly thinking of both himself and his other half.

That idea is retained in the speech of Diotima, although its mythical shell is cast away and its psychology is combined with Plato's theory of forms. One of Plato's key ideas is that the erotic drive that lies behind so much of what we do is both an expression of our self-love and our longing to become part of a larger community and to be in harmony with all that is beautiful in the world. The selfishness that underlies erotic love is not to be extirpated but to be educated.

We should contrast this conception of love with theories that call for us to cast aside all thought of own needs, or to make them secondary to those of others. Philosophers influenced by Kant's writings, for example, hold that we have a moral duty to promote the happiness of others but no moral duty to seek our own happiness, and that moral duties should always be given precedence over other options. Actions undertaken partly for one's own well-being are not morally principled, and so have less value than actions done for the sake of duty. Philosophers influenced by the writings of Mill and other utilitarians hold that one should sacrifice one's own well-being whenever one can maximize the good of others. Christian thinkers also give their highest praise to selfless service to others. Plato is far more comfortable with the self-centredness that is so common among human beings. His idea is not that one is to love oneself alone, or that one is to love oneself more than anyone else. The lover depicted by Aristophanes is as in love with his other half as he is responsive to his own need, and makes no important distinction between himself and his lover. Similarly, Plato, through the mouthpiece of Diotima, proposes that those best educated about erotic matters will love the whole world of beauty because they see this is what best serves their interest. The *Symposium* is a foundational text for all those who hold that love of others does not conflict with, but complements, love of self.

6

THE ASCENT TO GOODNESS

Socrates: Imagine people in an underground, cavelike dwelling, with an entrance open to the light, a long way off and as wide as the cave. They have been in it since childhood, their necks and legs in bonds so that they cannot move. They can see only what is in front of them, because their bonds make them unable to turn their heads around. Light comes from a fire burning far above and behind them. Between the fire and the prisoners is an elevated road, beside which imagine that a low wall has been built. It is like the screens that puppeteers set in front of people, above which they show their puppets. . . . Also imagine that there are people alongside the wall carrying all kinds artefacts that stick out above it – statues of men and other animals, made of stone, wood, and every material. . . .

Glaucon: A strange image you are describing, and strange prisoners.

Socrates: They are like us. (*Republic*, 514a–515a)

As the form of beauty lies at the heart of the *Symposium*, because it is the highest object of love, so the form of the good is at the centre of the *Republic*, because it is the highest object of knowledge. There are striking similarities between two key passages in each dialogue: In the *Symposium*, Diotima describes an 'education about erotic matters' in which a lover becomes increasingly aware of the wide range of beautiful objects that deserve his attention, and the beauty of what he loves increases as he proceeds, until he enjoys the vision of beauty itself. Correspondingly, in Book VII of the *Republic*, Socrates prescribes a course of studies in mathematics and science to be undertaken by anyone who wishes to become a philosopher. These studies bring the student into contact with increasingly real and diminishingly opaque objects, until he finally comes to an understanding of the most significant property of all, the form of the good.

The passage cited above comes from the beginning of Book VII (the *Republic* is divided into ten such 'books' – they might better be called 'chapters' or merely 'parts'). It describes the earliest stage of the progress that must be made not just by someone who aspires to become a philosopher, but by anyone who seeks a better life. The comparison made here between ourselves and prisoners in a cave is one of the most memorable and disturbing images in Plato's works. When Socrates says of the prisoners, 'They are like us', he means to refer not just to his interlocutors but to all human beings. We are all born to a kind of slavery or imprisonment and must struggle to win our way to a brighter and happier world, by overcoming a limitation in our conception of the world we live in. If we somehow manage to turn ourselves away from the wall of the cave – or, with someone's help, we are turned around – we will still be in dark surroundings, but at least our vision of the world will be less distorted and less subject to manipulation. If we do not recognize that the things we pay attention to are mere images, we will be taken advantage of by the people who are casting shadows on the wall of the cave.

Plato's *Republic* is, from start to finish, a political work. The very title (in Greek: *politeia*; the Latin equivalent, *res publica*, merely means 'public matter') emphasizes its civic character, and Socrates's analogy of the cave clearly has a political meaning. He goes on to say that if the prisoners are lucky enough to be released from their bondage, they will find it difficult to adjust to their changed orientation, and the force of habit will make them think they were better off when they were facing the wall of the cave, on which they could so easily make out familiar objects. The bright light of the fire within the cave will hurt their eyes, and they must be forced not to flee back to their condition of bondage. If the former prisoners are now dragged out of the cave, it will again take some time before they can adjust to the greater amount of light, and so they must begin their explorations of the natural world by studying the stars and the moon during the night, and the shadows cast by the sun during the day. But eventually they will be able to look at the sky in full daylight, and recognize the great importance of the sun to all living things. They will fully understand how much better their lives are. If they ever return to the cave, to help those who live there, they will have to go through another period of adjustment. The prisoners in the cave will at first be able to identify the shadows on the wall better than they, and will have nothing but disdain for anyone who claims to have seen a better world.

Although the initial hostility of the cave-dwellers to those who would free them is an allegorical reference to the common Athenian reaction to Socrates, we should not take Plato to mean that there will inevitably be hostile relationships between ordinary people and those who have acquired an understanding of the world's most important properties. The *Republic* depicts a hypothetical political community composed of philosophers and non-philosophers in which there is great harmony and mutual appreciation. Its main interlocutors are Adeimantus, Glaucon (these are the names of Plato's brothers) and Socrates. His brothers were not philosophers, but despite this difference from Socrates in their initial orientation, they all agree that there is an important role for those who have studied the forms – and particularly the form of the good – to play in civic life, and that this will be recognized by all citizens, when social conditions foster amicable relations.

The form of the good, Socrates says, is analogous to the sun.

Everything in the visible world depends for its existence and its perceptibility on the sun's warmth and light. Similarly, all the forms depend on the good for their being and their intelligibility. These are perplexing claims, but presumably Plato is suggesting that we can best understand the structure of the cosmos by seeing it as a good arrangement – one that is balanced, orderly and harmonious. At any rate, the eponymous speaker of the *Timaeus* (written some time after the *Republic*) proposes that the world can be viewed as the construction of a divine demi-urge who has transformed it into an organized and orderly condition by looking to the eternal forms and creating close approximations to them. The observable world, according to Timaeus, is far from perfect, but the considerable order it has reveals it to be the product of a mind who designed it to be as good as was allowed by the defective nature of the materials from which it is constructed. That is one reason why Plato might think it a matter of vital importance to understand what the form of goodness is: doing so will enable us to have a fuller appreciation of the imperfect orderliness of our visible cosmos, because we will understand the perfect model after which it was patterned by a divine agent.

Plato is perhaps also encouraged to think that the form of the good is of the greatest importance because of the way goodness figures in our ordinary practical thinking and endeavours. Although we rarely stop to think about the ultimate goals served by the actions we undertake, Plato assumes that we are implicitly guided by assumptions we make about the good we are doing for ourselves, our friends and family, or our fellow citizens. In this respect, goodness plays an even more important role in our lives than beauty. *Some* of what we do might be described as fine, or noble or beautiful. But not everything we undertake can be characterized in this way. When we stay fit and healthy, for example, we do so because we assume that it is good for us to do so, but we do not have to assume that health is noble or beauti-ful. Similarly, when we seek innocent enjoyments and pleasures, we take that to be a good thing, even if what we enjoy is not noble or beautiful. These facts about the important place goodness has in the justification of our actions presumably encourage Plato to embrace the hypothesis that the greatest object of philosophical study – and the pinnacle of the ascent from the cave to the open air – is the form of goodness.

The whole structure of the *Republic* rests on this hypothesis. The dialogue is an inquiry into the nature of justice, and the problem it seeks to solve is whether justice is *good*. Plato seems to be assuming that it is not enough that a state of affairs be just. Being a just person must be good or its claim on us will be thrown into doubt. This thesis, which Socrates seeks to demonstrate in the *Republic*, is certainly open to question, and Plato must realize this; otherwise he would not have taken the trouble to write a lengthy and complex work to establish it. One of the memorable interlocutors of the dialogue, a teacher of rhetoric named Thrasymachus, argues against that thesis in Book I; and Glaucon and Adeimantus add further details, in Book II, to support him. Plato is implicitly suggesting that we cannot hope to resolve this disagreement until we arrive at a fuller understanding of what goodness is. That seems completely reasonable: after all, how can we determine whether justice is good for someone, until we have clarified what it is for something to be good?

Nonetheless, very little is said in the *Republic* – at least explicitly – about what goodness is. The question is broached several pages before Socrates proposes the analogy of the cave. He points out that many people identify being good with being pleasant, but they cannot be right because there are bad pleasures (pleasures that are bad for someone to experience), and it would be nonsense to suppose that something can be both bad for someone to experience and at the same time good for him.

Socrates also considers the proposal that goodness should be defined as knowledge. But he makes short work of that idea by noting that knowledge is always knowledge of something. So, if we are to equate goodness with knowing something, we must also say what the object of that knowledge is. The answer cannot be: goodness. For goodness is precisely what we are trying to understand.

Having quickly dismissed these two possible ways of defining goodness – goodness as pleasure and goodness as knowledge – Socrates proposes that we come to a better understanding of it by way of analogy, and that good occupies the same position in the realm of the forms that the sun occupies in the visible world. This tells us something about how important goodness is, but it is not a theory about what goodness is. The *Republic* therefore lacks the very thing that Socrates says is most important to have: an account of goodness. Perhaps we should not be entirely surprised by this, for there is a similar silence in the *Symposium*, which tells us, in the voice of Diotima, that beauty is the highest object of the lover's ascent, but does not offer a theory about what beauty is.

No other work of Plato proposes a definition of either beauty or goodness. In the *Republic* Socrates offers definitions of justice and several other virtues, but not of the good. Nonetheless, we get a brief hint of what goodness might be in a late dialogue, the *Philebus*. This work begins with a question that rehearses the two alternatives canvassed in the *Republic* about what goodness might be: is good to be equated with pleasure or with knowledge? The response worked out over the course of the dialogue by Socrates and Protarchus is that the good should not be identified solely with either of these two psychological states, for neither one taken by itself could make a human life fully worth living. No matter how much pleasure we had, we would be missing something desirable if we lacked knowledge; and similarly, no matter how much knowledge we had, our lives would be the worse for lacking pleasure. What makes for a good life is not just one or the other of these two conditions, but the combination of the two, properly proportioned and measured. More generally, Socrates and Protarchus agree that whatever is complex will be made good when its diverse components are brought together in a harmonious and balanced way, and so what constitutes the good for any such object is precisely that state of proper order. Goodness consists in balanced unification of the diverse parts of a thing.

Goodness as harmony, measure or unity is at work throughout Socrates's depiction, in the *Republic*, of an ideal political community as one in which harmony and a sense of unity prevails among all citizens. The greatest good for any city, he says, is that which binds it together and prevents the development of rival factions. Similarly, the greatest good for a single individual is to be psychologically unified. Being a unified whole is not only good for the thing that is unified – to be unified is precisely what being good is.

Goodness, then, is a close kin to beauty, since Plato undoubtedly assumes that a thing's balance, harmony, proportion and unity make it beautiful. Aesthetics and ethics – the study of beauty and morality – must be studied together because the objects they seek to understand are so closely related that it is difficult to tell them apart. Plato even leaves open the possibility that we will discover that they are the same thing.

Plato's hypothesis that goodness is a single property, akin to beauty, central to any understanding of the cosmos, and our principal guide to ethical and political deliberation, was accepted in its entirety by Plotinus (third century AD) and his school, which exerted a profound influence on one of the greatest Christian philosophers, Augustine, in the fourth to fifth centuries. God, as conceived by Christianity, plays the role of Plato's form of the good, but is a supreme mind and not an abstract property. In some ways, Christianity is more intelligible than Platonism, because it is easier for us to understand how a mind might be responsible for the existence of an orderly cosmos than to see how the property of goodness can by itself have any causal power. But from Plato's perspective, Christianity or any other religion that fails to acknowledge the forms as the ultimate reality makes little sense. A divine mind must be guided by some model of perfection outside itself. The form of the good is what a divine creator looks to, as a standard for its governance of the universe. That form, then, not God, is the ultimate explanation of the order of the universe.

Other schools of philosophy pose different objections to Plato's theory of the good. He argues in many of his dialogues against the identification of goodness with pleasure, but several decades after his death the Epicurean school established itself in Athens, and won many adherents to its equation of well-being with pleasure. Epicureanism did not endure for more than a few centuries, and the Christian identification of goodness with God, a close cousin of Platonism, dominated the medieval period. But many philosophers of the modern period revived the Epicurean thesis that goodness is pleasure, and this way of thinking culminated in the utilitarianism of Jeremy Bentham and John Stuart Mill in the nineteenth century. Their famous formula – the greatest happiness of the greatest number – is, in one way, a modern reincarnation of Platonism, because it agrees with Plato that goodness is a single property and that we should look ultimately to the good as our guide to making decisions. But the utilitarians depart from Plato in several ways: they identify goodness with happiness or pleasure rather than harmonious order, and they do not endorse Plato's idea that goodness is responsible for the orderly arrangement of the visible cosmos. Utilitarianism is a wholly practical philosophy, whereas Plato seeks not only a guide to practice but a framework for understanding everything in and beyond the visible universe.

One other alternative to Plato's theory of the good is found in Aristotle, who rejects the assumption that goodness is a single, unified property. He holds that many different kinds of thing are good, but there is no one property that makes them all good. The disagreement between Plato and Aristotle has hardly been settled. In the early part of the twentieth century, G. E. Moore, an English philosopher, argued that although goodness cannot be defined, it is, as Plato claimed, the property that we must look to in all that we do. It exists independently of our desires, but if we think clearly enough about it, we can intuitively recognize which things have that property and which do not. Moore's views about the good played a central role in twentieth-century moral philosophy, and some of his opponents took a position not far from Aristotle's. They argue that to talk about what is good – just plain good – is nonsense. We can sensibly talk about what is good *for* someone, as well as about good poems, good food, or good card games. What makes these things good is not a single property, but something different in each case.

Plato would reply that in each of the diverse things we call good, we find harmony, proportion or balance. Good food, for example, is part of a balanced diet, beautiful works of art satisfy our sense of proportion, and good card games must be neither too easy nor too difficult. Plato's conception of the good is difficult to evaluate, but it is not blatant nonsense. Like so many other elements of his philosophy, it is neither obviously false nor obviously true. That is one reason why Plato is still worth reading.

THE DEFINITION OF JUSTICE

Socrates: It was . . . a sort of image of justice, this principle that it is right for someone who is, by nature, a shoemaker to practise shoemaking and nothing else, for a carpenter to practise carpentry, and so on. . . . Yet in truth . . . justice is not concerned with doing what is one's own on the outside but rather on the inside . . . so that one prevents each element within oneself from doing what belongs to another . . . One rules oneself, puts oneself in order, becomes one's own friend, and harmonizes the three elements. . . . (*Republic*, 443c–d)

Socrates: . . . to produce justice is to establish the elements in the soul in a natural relation of controlling and being controlled by one another, whereas to produce injustice is to establish a relation of ruling and being ruled by another that is contrary to nature . . . (*Republic*, 444d)

The allegory of the cave occupies a central position in the *Republic*, since it encapsulates, within a single striking image and narrative, important elements of Plato's metaphysics, epistemology, ethics and political philosophy. To appreciate its meaning fully, one must see the role it plays within the framework of the whole dialogue. It is part of an elaborate argumentative structure, for the *Republic*, despite its diversity of topics, is a unified and artistic whole dedicated to a single task: the elaboration of a theory of justice and the demonstration that justice is the greatest good a person can possess. We saw in the previous chapter that, for Plato, a thing's goodness consists in its unification of diverse parts. The *Republic* is itself an instance of that harmonization of components, and perhaps Plato counts it in favour of his theory of goodness that it corresponds to the standard by which we evaluate the design of all human artefacts, including poems, statues, philosophical dialogues, tables and houses.

Many of the *Republic*'s books are more or less continuous with the others, but the first of them is marked off from the others by the dialogue's interlocutors themselves: their discussion of justice, they say at the beginning of Book II, must make a fresh start, because it tried to establish the goodness of justice without first giving an account of what justice is. That project – the definition of justice – then becomes the preoccupation of the whole work. Socrates proclaims at the end of Book IV that the right definition has been found, although it emerges that it requires more elaboration. The central idea is that the human soul is composed of three parts – reason, spirit and appetite – and that justice consists in each part playing its natural and proper role. Reason must be established as the master of the other two. Plato realizes that his theory will be convincing only if he gives us a fuller picture of what it means for reason, or spirit, or appetite to rule the soul. He accomplishes this by giving us portraits of people who exemplify these psychological traits. At the centre of the *Republic* lies his depiction of the person whose life he claims is most fully governed by reason – the philosopher who has achieved an understanding of the form of the good. In the later books of the *Republic*, he rounds out his theory by giving us portraits of someone ruled by spirit, and several portraits of people ruled by appetite.

Socrates and his interlocutors never doubt that treating other people justly brings with it all sorts of benefits for the people who are so treated. The question on their minds is whether being a just person is of any benefit to the just person himself. At the beginning of Book II, Glaucon and Adeimantus play devil's advocate: they argue that no one wants to be just for its own sake, and rightly so, because abiding by laws and social norms that protect people from murder, theft and other injustices places a limitation on us that we would all rightly prefer, at least at times, to overthrow. If we could secretly get away with injustice and suffer none of the usual consequences – legal punishment, social ostracism, and the like – we would pay it little regard precisely because it is a restriction that we normally accept only as the price we have to pay to expect just treatment from others. To show that this conception of justice is misguided, Socrates argues that justice is, by itself, a great good – so great, in fact, that it is better to be a just person than an unjust person, regardless of the social consequences.

Notice a defect in the case Glaucon and Adeimantus offer in defence of acting unjustly whenever one can get away with it. They merely say that this is what nearly anyone *would* do. But Socrates is asking whether this is something we *should* do. Admittedly, an unjust person can satisfy many of his illicit desires and feel all sorts of pleasures that are unknown to those who are just. But that would count in favour of being an unjust person only on the assumption that it is always good for someone to satisfy his desires and to feel pleasure, regardless of the content of his desires and the objects of his pleasure. Book IX of the *Republic* contains a conception of pleasure that takes the value of a pleasure to depend on the value of that pleasure's object. If it can be shown that being a just person is harmful to one's soul, then whatever pleasure people get from acting unjustly is a bad pleasure for them to experience.

Some philosophers, especially philosophers of the modern period, believe that Plato has gone astray in the *Republic*, because he seems to presuppose that justice is a quality worth acquiring only if it is in one's interest to do so. Is it not enough justification for an act that it is the just thing to do? And is it not enough justification that it does good to those who are treated justly? They question why it should be important to show of a just action that it is good for us as well. These doubts about Plato's project are often raised by followers of Kant, who argued that a moral person will do what is morally right merely because that is his duty. If justice requires us to keep a promise we have made, that is all the reason we should need. Perhaps it will be in our interest to keep the promise, or perhaps not. That should not matter. We must keep the promise only because it would be morally wrong not to.

But we should not assume too quickly that Plato's attempt to find self-interested reasons for being just shows that self-interest is the only motive of which he could approve. The *Republic* recognizes that self-interest is a powerful motive and that if it is not guided by a proper understanding of what is in one's interest, the consequences for oneself and others will be disastrous. The question 'what is good for me?' is one that we may legitimately ask. It is a question that can be answered only if we address ourselves to broader questions: What is good for anyone? What is the nature of goodness? Philosophy must not evade those questions.

We need not find fault with the Kantian thesis that good people conscientiously abide by general principles of moral rightness, for that creates no difficulty for Plato's project. In fact, abiding by moral principles requires a proper understanding of the good. Those principles require us to do what is good for others (and leave room for us to pursue our own good). But if we have a defective notion of what is good, we will be unable to fulfil our moral duty to help others achieve their good. Our responsibility, after all, is to seek not what merely seems to be good for them, but what really is good.

The principal burden of the *Republic* is to show that even if there were no afterlife, we would still have the strongest possible reason to become and remain just people simply because of the great good that justice is in this life. Plato believes that we are making a horrible mistake if our love of justice is mediated by our expectation or hope that we will judged favourably in the afterlife. That thesis brings him into conflict with the conviction that many people have had throughout the Christian era. Plato is a deeply religious thinker, but he shares with secular philosophers the hypothesis that the moral virtues are grounded in a rational appreciation of their great value, and that they need no further grounding in the rewards of an afterlife. His thesis that the cosmos is an orderly image of a transcendent order and that we can be better off when the soul is separated from the body at death make him an ally of Christian thought. But his conviction that whether the soul endures or not, this life is worth living, if we are just and have the other moral virtues, brings him closer to secularism than to many religious philosophies.

Justice can be better understood, according to Socrates, if we reflect on what it is for a city to be just, and then apply the lessons we learn to the individual. Just as we can more easily identify letters when they are large than when they are small, so we can better clarify our ideas about justice by first asking what it is for a whole city to be just, and then asking what it is for an individual to be just. (The Greek word *polis* is often translated 'city' or 'city-state' to remind us that these political units were far smaller and more cohesive than modern nation-states.) This methodological counsel plays a profound role throughout the remainder of the dialogue. The *Republic* henceforth becomes an exercise in utopian thinking. Plato is asking what the best possible political community is, because even if we do not bring it into existence, and do not bring the cities in which we live one inch closer to justice, we will in any case have in our mind's eye a model of what a just individual is, and that can guide our practical thinking in the real world, no matter what our political circumstances are.

According to his conception of the ideal city, jobs are to be performed by those well suited to excel in those positions. As the passage cited at the beginning of the chapter prescribes, the shoemakers should stick to making shoes, carpenters to carpentry.

This simple idea contains the germs of a conception of justice, especially when it is applied to the individual soul. For Socrates soon suggests that the ideal city will have both a specialized military force and a specialized political class – two groups of citizens peculiarly suited, by nature and training, to defend the city against external and internal dangers, and to make decisions that affect the well-being of all. The ideal city would contain three major cooperative groups: an economic class, a military class, and a governing class. The justice of a city lies in the principle that each citizen should do his own job and no one else's, and in this way contribute to the city whatever he is well suited to provide.

This idea will shed light on what it is to be a just individual only if there is a threefold structure within each of us that corresponds in some way to the three classes of the ideal city – the workers, the soldiers and the rulers. Socrates argues that we can find within the human soul precisely that structure. Each of us has physical needs and drives – for food, drink, sexual satisfaction, and the like. These form the appetitive part of the soul, which corresponds to the economic class of the city. Each of us is sensitive to how we stand in relation to others: we strive to excel in competitions, we hunger after the recognition that comes with status, we are angered by slights. These vulnerabilities form the spirited element of the soul. Finally, we are all able to reflect on the considerations that should be taken into account when we make decisions, and to arrive at a conclusion about what to do that reflects the weight that we have assigned to each of the relevant factors. That is the reasoning part of the soul. So if the analogy between city and soul is to guide us, we will say that the justice of an individual consists in each part of the soul remaining within its proper boundaries and thereby making its best contribution to the rest of the soul. Justice is each part of the soul doing its own job. And since it is the job of reason to govern the soul, justice can also be defined as the rule of reason.

In the *Phaedrus* Socrates uses a striking image that conveys this conception of the human soul as a thing divided into three components: each of us is like a team composed of a chariot driver and his two winged horses, one horse being unruly, the other more compliant. The image conveys the inherent difficulty of managing the soul so that it acts as a single effective and smoothly operating team. Horses are powerful animals with a mind of their own, and it requires great discipline and skill to train them so that they gracefully carry out the commands of their driver. A good driver needs to know where he should be going, and must not let his horses make this decision for him. In order to reach that point, he must know how to make decisions that are independent of the pushes and pulls of his horses, and he must be on such good terms with those horses that they will uncomplainingly take him where he wants to go. Reason, in other words, will get us nowhere entirely on its own − it must enlist the support of the other components of our psychology, or its operations will be idle. But through reasoning we can take into account something other than our own drives and inclinations, when we resolve what to do. We can look to just relations among citizens, to beauty, to goodness, and decide to shape the rest of our souls so that we are effective in our pursuit of these goals. One can easily see why Plato thinks it is a great good to be a just person.

A threefold analysis of human psychology is familiar to readers of Freud, and there are affinities as well as differences between his ideas about the mind and Plato's. The id, like Platonic appetite, is the repository of our sexual instincts, and for both Freud and Plato there is an erotic aspect to nearly every aspect of our lives. But appetite also houses hunger, thirst, and our desire for material possessions. The Freudian ego is the part of us that faces reality; negotiates, often quite poorly, the conflicts within the soul; and decides how to achieve one's goals. Similarly, reason, as Plato conceives it, is the soul's decision-maker, and like Freud he thinks that it has great difficulty managing the powerful non-rational forces at work within us. But here there is also a great difference between Plato and Freud, because Plato thinks that reality contains a supreme guide to decision-making – the eternal forms – whereas Freud's psychology is not tethered to a metaphysical or ethical theory. Their conceptions of the third part of the soul also exhibit important similarities and differences. Freud's super-ego represents the strict and painful commands of one's parents and one's society's moral code, and it tends to make demands that require costly renunciations of pleasure. Plato's spirit is likewise other-directed, being the seat of such social emotions as anger and our desire to be admired. But he regards it as a natural ally of reason rather than its tormentor. Plato shares with Freud a pessimism about whether there can be a social world in which all people are at peace with themselves and others, but this is tempered by his thesis that human reason, at its best, is fit to understand the world and can find its place among the divine forms, the divinely ordered visible cosmos, and a more just social order.

Every human being, according to Plato, has the capacity to reason and to make decisions. But not every human being has trained himself so that he has a basis for making decisions that is independent of the promptings of our emotional and appetitive nature. To be governed by reason, as Plato conceives of it, is to be able to reflect on our psychological tendencies and the social norms that happen to prevail in our communities and to decide which of them to accept and nourish. To do that, one must ask the questions that Socrates asked, and one must develop answers to those questions. That is why Plato's argument that justice is a great good is not complete until he has used the allegory of the cave to convey the idea that we must govern our lives by developing an understanding of what is good. Justice consists in the rule of reason, but we do not fully appreciate what the rule of reason is until we recognize the standards by which reason should rule. For Plato then, the search for an understanding of justice eventually leads to a knowledge of the highest form – the property of goodness.

8

UTOPIA

Socrates: . . . in founding the city, we are not looking to make any one group in it outstandingly happy, but to make the whole city so, as far as possible. For we thought that in such a city we would best be able to find justice . . . (*Republic*, 420b)

Socrates: Are they [who live in a democracy] free, and is the city full of freedom and freedom of speech, and is there licence in it to do whatever one wants? . . . It is likely to be the most beautiful constitution . . . being embroidered with every sort of character. . . . There is no requirement to hold office in this city, even if you are qualified to do so, nor to be governed if you do not want to be . . . Isn't it magnificent how it . . . gives no thought to the sorts of practices someone went in for before he entered politics, and honours him if he merely says that he is well disposed to the people? . . . It seems to be a pleasant constitution – anarchic and variegated, assigning a sort of equality to equals and unequals alike. (*Republic*, 557b–558c)

Athenian: It is necessary for human beings to establish laws and to live according to laws, or else to differ not at all from beasts that are savage in every way. The reason is this, that no human being has a nature that can develop so that he knows what is beneficial for human beings in their political organization and then, having understood it, is always able and willing to achieve what is best. For in the first place it is difficult to understand that a truly expert political art must care for the public good, not private good. . . . And second even if someone adequately grasps, by his understanding of the art of politics, that these things are naturally so, and then governs a city autocratically, without being held accountable, he would never be able to stick to his conviction and to continue, throughout his life, to give priority to fostering the common good of the city. . . . His mortal nature will always impel him to overreach and to put his own good above others'. . . . Yet if, through divine good fortune, a human being should be born who is competent by nature and capable of filling such an office, he would have no need of rulers over him. For no law or arrangement is superior to knowledge, and it is not right for reason to be subordinate to or a slave to anything, but it must govern all things. . . . (*Laws*, 874e–875c)

After writing the *Republic*, Plato composed two more dialogues that address political issues: the *Statesman* (about one tenth the size of the *Republic*) and the *Laws* (his longest work, about twenty per cent longer than the *Republic*). Had he written only the *Republic*, his stature as a political philosopher would be indisputable; it is unquestionably his most important political work. But if one neglects his later thinking, one might be tempted to think that he had no interest in improving the day-to-day functioning of imperfect political communities. The *Republic* depicts an ideal city that Plato knew was unlikely ever to be established. It enters the terrain of utopian politics only because doing so will illuminate the value of being a good person regardless of the kind of city one lives in. But in the *Laws* Plato shows his deep interest in what can be achieved by ordinary human beings faced with the task of ruling themselves. He devotes a large part of this dialogue to drafting detailed laws and prescribing precise punishments for their violation — as well as articulating the broad philosophical justification for those legislative details. Much of this material could have been appropriated piecemeal for the reform of already existing political communities. Plato insists several times in the *Republic* that the ideal city is achievable, and contains nothing inherently at odds with human nature or social relations. But in the *Laws* he gives the details of a second-best city that is far easier to achieve.

Among the many remarkable features of the ideal city described in the *Republic* (sometimes called Kallipolis – 'fine city') are the radical departures Socrates proposes from familiar political and social institutions. Athens was a direct democracy: all citizens (free adult males born of citizen parents) had the right to attend and vote in the assembly that made the major decisions of civic life. Many offices were filled by lot to ensure that rule would be equally shared. By contrast, Kallipolis is governed by those who have successfully passed all of the intellectual tests established by the city's founders, and have shown by their closely observed behaviour that they are wholeheartedly and impartially devoted to the well-being and happiness of all citizens. Once they pass these rigorous tests, they are given unlimited and unchecked power; having shown themselves to be entirely trustworthy and wise, no institutions circumscribe their authority. Nonetheless, there are significant institutional safeguards against the most common sources of misgovernment, for these philosopher-kings are deprived of all significant forms of wealth and property. That not only frees them from the burdens of ownership, it also assures other citizens that the power of the rulers cannot be used for their own enrichment.

No less radical is Socrates's admission of women to the ruling and soldiering classes and his abolition of the traditional family among them. They live not in separate households but in communal quarters, because that will foster a greater sense of community among them. Marriages between men and women will be arranged with a view to producing the best offspring, and children will be raised not by their biological parents but by specialists in childcare. That will free women of these classes from the burdens of childrearing. No longer confined to the household, they will be able to use their talents to serve the whole community.

The guiding principle of this ideal city is that anyone who is qualified to occupy a position that benefits the city should be admitted to that office. Socrates argues that even if women are, as a group, inferior in talent to men, exceptional women should be welcomed into all areas of social life, including the governance of the city. Some women, therefore, will have absolute power over nearly all men.

Socrates is hostile to any social institution that encourages citizens to be partial in their allegiances, and he assumes that kinship groups foster such partiality by creating divisions between insiders and outsiders. Justice in the polis requires the impartial treatment of all: the good of each individual is just as important as the good of any other. Philosophers are to rule, courageous warriors are to protect the city, and skilled craftsmen and farmers are to secure its material well-being because all jobs should be filled in a way that serves the common good, not just the good of job-holders. Since justice requires impartiality, and the traditional family deflects us from an equal regard for all, it is best that some other system of producing the next generation be put in place.

Plato wants Kallipolis to be a feasible ideal and so he does not propose the abolition of the family in all classes. All successful social institutions must eventually win the approval of those who participate in them (however reluctant they may be, at first, to enter them). Most people want to live in families and to have their own material possessions – land, houses, money and the like. They are naturally disposed to build their lives around the pleasures of food, sex and material ownership – just as soldiering types love honour and victory, and philosophical types love learning and reasoned discourse. In Kallipolis, these three groups of distinctive tendencies will thrive, but accommodating the natural householding dispositions of ordinary people comes at a

price: members of the economic class, because of their partiality
to family and their attachment to their possessions, cannot have
the objective regard for the common good that ideal rulers ought
to have, and so cannot be among the city's decision-makers.
Socrates assumes that they will not be offended or dissatisfied by
their exclusion from the deliberative offices of the city. And it
has been true over the course of history that most people who
lack political power are not discontented with their position, so
long as they are confident that they are well governed and will
remain so.

Two other aspects of Kallipolis are offensive to modern liberal
democratic sensibilities: it makes use of official lies, and it censors
poetry. In Kallipolis, citizens are told that they are all born of the
same parent – the nurturing earth that is their homeland – and
that the metals that make up their bodies (in some cases gold, in
others silver, in others bronze) determine where their talents lie
and the social roles they should play. Plato was convinced that the
widespread acceptance of certain myths creates a social cohesion
stronger than the ties that reason can forge on its own. Reason,
properly educated, will tell each citizen that justice is in his self-
interest, and that will incline him to fulfil his duty and play his
assigned civic role; but since we are not made of reason alone, it
must be supplemented by myth, if we are to be as fully devoted
as we can be to our city, our fellow citizens, and our social roles.
Lies enter civic life at a second point: the eugenic programme by
which the most talented men and women are matched with each
other misleads couples into thinking that a lot determined their
pairing.

That lies must never be told under any circumstances is a
thesis that few philosophers have embraced – Augustine and
Kant are the most notable exceptions. The more moderate thesis
most would accept is that state officials should lie only in exceptional circumstances, and that even in these cases deliberately
misleading others ought to go against their grain. Plato sides with
the moderates. He realizes that ruling well sometimes requires a

ruler to do what he would otherwise prefer not to do. He also embraces a broader thesis: people who have a philosophical nature do not strive after power over others and do not like the business of giving commands. They would rather engage in reasoned discourse about the nature of the most important properties. Those who have discovered the world outside the cave and have seen the sun are reluctant to return to the cave and to free others from their bondage, even though this is what justice requires. The philosopher's reluctance to exercise power over others is one of the factors that Socrates thinks qualifies him to do precisely that. We are rightly loath to be governed by people who relish power for its own sake.

In the *Laws*, the unnamed Athenian visitor to Crete who is the dialogue's principal interlocutor insists that laws should, so far as possible, be introduced by preambles that explain their rational basis. Citizens are not to be treated as unthinking creatures who must be ordered about like animals or slaves. Laws are instituted in order to achieve worthwhile goals; those goals must be set forth clearly, and so too must the way in which legislation serves them. The Athenian is not claiming that laws are legitimate only if they have the unanimous *consent* of those who are governed by them; but they must be such that those who are governed by them can understand why they are needed. A well-governed political community must be an 'open society' (to use the twentieth-century philosopher Karl Popper's phrase). What lies are told must be the rare exception rather than the rule. In fact, the interlocutors of the *Laws* do not envisage any need for lies. The good but non-ideal society it depicts has no need of the myth of the metals or of eugenic lies.

But Plato shows no sympathy for an idea that has been an important part of liberal thought – that restrictions on speech should be as few as possible, and that artistic expression in particular must be placed beyond the purview of politics. One of the most shocking aspects of the *Republic* lies in the radical restrictions that are placed on the poets of Kallipolis, and the expurgation of many lines of Homer and other writers whose poetry was the core of the education of all literate Greeks in Plato's time. Homer depicts the gods as liars, thieves and murderers. Because of him and other poets, it was commonly believed that one need only make proper sacrifices to the gods in order to evade divine punishment for one's misdeeds. Conventional Greek religion, Plato believes, is a corrupting force in civic life, because it reinforces the common belief that injustice can often be in one's interest. Just as we have come to rely on the modern state to forbid false advertising in the sale of food and drugs, so Kallipolis does not allow an open 'market place of ideas' regarding what is good and bad, right and wrong.

The *Laws* is no less restrictive than the *Republic* in its regulation of poetry and other forms of speech. Plato's assumption is that false claims about how we should behave and what we should ultimately value can tap into the appetitive and spirited parts of our psychology, and they will not lose their hold on us merely by exposure to the light of reason. The political community must be governed by reasoned discourse (that is the point of having preambles to legislation), but reasoned discourse will not necessarily prevail when it has to compete with the forces of un-reason. Frank and open discussion has an important role to play in both politics and philosophy – Socrates certainly insists upon this in the *Gorgias* – but only among those who are prepared to benefit from it.

The good but non-ideal city depicted in the *Laws* (it is at certain points referred to as Magnesia) does away with many of the institutions that make Kallipolis a radical departure from ordinary political communities. All citizens are members of households: they each own the same amount of land, marry, have children, and are trained as soldiers. Women still help with the defence of the city, and in this way Magnesia reaffirms the thesis of the *Republic* that women should play a far larger role in civic life than was ordinarily the case in Greek cities. There is no division of citizens into three classes, as there is in the *Republic*; no elite composed of philosophers specially trained to exercise absolute power. Instead, those who serve on the most important councils and occupy the most powerful offices are selected by the vote of all citizens. The framework of civic life is structured by an elaborate set of laws, and the constitution makes it difficult or impossible to change them. The power of all citizens, even those who hold high office, is highly restricted by legal prohibitions. No one is above the law; every official is to be held accountable, should he misuse his office.

Magnesia is presented not as the best possible city, but as an approximation to the best. It would be ideal, the Athenian says, for the citizens to have all things in common, as friends do; that would mean the complete exclusion of what is private – property and family – throughout the whole city. That is the same ideal proposed by Socrates for Kallipolis, and so Plato's conception of what makes a city best – maximal unity – does not change. All Magnesians are allowed to have private property, but wealth above a certain limit is prohibited, and because the material resources of wealthy and poor citizens are not radically different, there is no hostility between them. The citizens achieve a strong sense of unity because all receive the same public education, all serve together in the army, all are welcome (some are required) to participate in elections, and all take part in the same religious, dramatic and athletic festivals.

What has happened to the idea that philosophers should rule? Perhaps Plato changed his mind about that radical thesis, because he came to realize that giving absolute power to anyone, no matter how carefully scrutinized and trained, is too dangerous. Human nature is inherently corruptible by power. A different interpretation is also possible. Just as Plato uses Magnesia to show how a less than ideal degree of unity can be achieved even when the traditional household is preserved, so he may also be using this second-best city to show how philosophical reason can govern a city even when rulers are democratically elected by citizens or chosen by lot. Magnesia is governed by a detailed set of

laws difficult for citizens to alter. Everything they do is limited by
the city's constitution. Plato's philosophy designed this constitution. His conception of goodness as harmony stands behind the
goal of social unity that animates this second-best city's legal
system. The leading officers of the city are not trained to be
dialecticians who study the form of the good, but Plato must
count that as one of the features of Magnesia that makes it less
than ideal. This defect is mitigated when, in the final book of the
Laws, the Athenian advocates the formation of a special council
of leading figures whose education is philosophical. Called the
'Nocturnal Council' because it meets shortly before sunrise, it
fosters the growth of philosophical reason and its application to
questions of governance, even though its powers are left unspec-
ified. In Magnesia, philosophy plays an important role in civic
life, even though there are no philosopher-kings.

Plato's most fundamental thesis is that some place must be
found in any well-governed city for those who have a deeper
than normal understanding of and appreciation for what is good
and just. In Kallipolis, those insights reside in exquisitely trained
philosophers who are entrusted with absolute power over all
civic matters. In Magnesia those insights reside in several different places: in the constitutional framework that has been
informed by philosophical reasoning; in the investigations of the
Nocturnal Council; and in the ability of ordinary citizens, when
they are not driven apart by economic need or gross inequality,
but brought together by their common education and social
practices, to pick out a few people of exemplary character to fill
high offices.

What Plato dislikes about democracy is that it neglects the
need cities have to be guided by knowledge. In fact, its hall-
marks – equality and the freedom to live as one likes – conflict
with the need to base civic life on an understanding of what is
good and just. Democracy hates hierarchy, and insists that all free
citizens share equally in power, regardless of their character and
understanding. It hates restrictions on choice, and so places limits

on what the legal system can achieve by means of good laws. There are many ways for defenders of democracy to respond to Plato's attack, and he has certainly not had the last word on this subject. But it would be a mistake to pay no heed to his critique of democracy. Successful political communities must find a place for knowledge – not only for technical expertise, but for the kind of knowledge that understands the ends that are most worth pursuing.

9

ATHEISM AND OTHER DANGERS

Athenian (speaking to an imaginary young man who chastises the gods for neglecting human affairs): The supervisor of the universe has put all things together with a view to the preservation and excellence of the whole, and each part acts and reacts as best it can in the appropriate way. Rulers have been assigned to each of these parts, even for the smallest aspect of their actions and reactions, and these rulers have achieved their goals down to the last detail. One of these parts is yours . . . and it constantly seeks and looks to the whole, even though it is extremely small. It has escaped your notice . . . that everything is generated so that the life of the universe is a happy existence. It has not come about for you, but you for it . . . But you complain because you do not realize that what is best for you to do for the universe is best for you as well, because of the force of your common origin. (*Laws*, 903b–d)

Socrates was sentenced to death because he was judged to have violated the Athenian law against impiety, and although the works of Plato reflect his conviction that a deeply flawed city thereby killed the best man of his time, he never shows any doubt that it is appropriate for the political community to regulate religious behaviour and belief. His acceptance of civic authority over religious practices represents the conventional wisdom of his time and place, and many other times and places as well. Complete separation of church and state is an experiment that few political communities have undertaken, and the philosophical thesis that they ought to be separate, which has now become a staple of liberal political theory, would have been rejected not only by Plato but by nearly every other canonical thinker prior to the twentieth century.

In fact, it is perhaps misleading to speak as though state and church could be entirely separate realms, for the state must take some stand or other regarding religion. It does so even when it chooses to be equally protective of all religious practices. Consider, for example, the First Amendment of the Constitution of the United States, which bars Congress from prohibiting the 'free exercise' of religion. Religion is thereby given a special status in American life: although the freedom of American citizens is legally restricted in all sorts of ways, speech and action cannot be curtailed if they constitute the exercise of a religious practice, even if the majority thinks that those who engage in these religious practices are harming each other. Speaking in Plato's terms, we might say that the United States, like many other nations influenced by the liberal political tradition, protects the virtue of piety by assuring citizens that they will be unhindered in developing and exercising this habit of mind. If we ask why piety should be so protected, it is tempting to reply that it is a quality of great value.

Plato's Magnesia likewise protects the virtue of piety, but it does so by shaping the religious beliefs and practices of its citizens. To a large extent, the Athenian's prescriptions regarding religious practices in Magnesia are borrowed from the cultural traditions that prevailed in Athens and many other Greek cities of the ancient world. Plato's *Laws* does not invent religious institutions out of whole cloth. The Greeks publicly honoured their gods by means of a regular round of seasonal festivals, many of which featured dramatic, musical and athletic performances and competitions. They also maintained temples and shrines at public expense, for the recitation of prayers and the performance of sacrifices. Many people had, in addition, small shrines in their homes. The citizens of Magnesia will likewise spend much of their time out in the open with each other, celebrating in song and dance the arrival of new seasons, the harvesting of crops, and other events that they take to reveal the divine governance of the natural world.

The Athenian's endorsement of these traditional ways should not be regarded as an expression of Plato's willingness to leave traditional practices alone simply because they are traditional. As the *Republic* so clearly shows, Plato is willing to abolish or reform traditions, if he thinks he can improve on them. In the *Laws*, the Athenian proposes that private shrines be prohibited in Magnesia, because he wants all religious practices to fall under the purview of public scrutiny. What is he afraid of? Precisely what Socrates fears in the *Republic*: it is a common view in the Greek world that one can commit a crime and avoid divine punishment, if one privately makes amends by bribing the gods with prayers and sacrifices. It is a theme that unites Kallipolis and Magnesia that religion must be made to serve the common good as that good is perceived by a well-governed political community. Although Magnesia is less radical than Kallipolis in that it leaves the household intact and gives ordinary citizens an important role to play in political governance, it requires all citizens to adhere to a rational religion – a religion, in other words, that can be vindicated by philosophical argument. The Athenian believes that the gods do not protect wrongdoers, and he is convinced that the common good is undermined by those who think otherwise.

The idea that the gods can be bribed to intervene on behalf of one's private interests, contrary to the good of others, is the third of three pernicious doctrines that the Athenian proposes to banish from Magnesia. The first is the thesis that the gods do not exist. The second grants that they exist, but insists that they have no concern for human affairs. That second thesis attracted many Greek philosophers. It was propounded by Aristotle and the Epicurean school that arose soon after his death. But Plato is convinced not only that there is a divine 'supervisor of the universe' who, with the help of assistants, looks after 'the small-est details' of the world's operations, but that this god is not indifferent to human well-being and doles out rewards and pun-ishments in an afterlife. Plato's divine supervisors do not intercede in human affairs by performing miracles. They did not create the material from which the universe is composed, but merely trans-formed it so that it would provide a beautiful and inspiring setting for human beings. Worshipping them is an appropriate acknow-ledgement of the work they have done for us. We find echoes of Plato's religious philosophy in the Deism that flourished among thinkers like Thomas Jefferson and Benjamin Franklin in the sev-enteenth and eighteenth centuries. Against Christianity, deists held that religious truths are based entirely on reason, and they rejected the possibility of miraculous divine intervention.

The doctrines of atheism and divine indifference were embraced in Plato's age by a small handful of speculative thinkers, but not by the vast majority of ordinary people. Nonetheless, the Athenian does not want to leave it to chance that atheism and the doctrine of divine indifference will not win more adherents and eventually eat away at the common good. He believes that there are gods, that these gods care for human beings, that wide-spread failure to recognize these truths will harm the city, and that this failure might become widespread unless the city upholds these truths and persuades dissenters that they are mistaken. At least some of the citizens of Magnesia, he assumes, are capable of recognizing the cogency of arguments that affirm the existence of divine beings who care about human happiness and are eager to help us, provided we do our part by properly governing our-selves. Those arguments are set forth in Book X of the *Laws*. Furthermore, he suggests at one point that the *Laws* should be preserved as the founding document of this new city, so that all its citizens can read it and appeal to it as the framework for their thinking. They will believe in caring gods not merely because it has long been customary to do so, but because a theology of divine providence is backed by reason.

The argument for the existence of divine beings is that there could be no motion in the world unless there is a kind of entity that can move both itself and other things. Only souls, not soulless matter, can play that role. Souls not only have the ability to impart motion but are also capable of planning, designing and overseeing things. The beautifully organized structure of the material cosmos can best be explained as the product not of randomness or sheer force but of powerful, though not omnipotent, governing souls. The heavenly spheres are not unconscious matter, but are moved by intelligence. These are gods and it is appropriate to worship them, as pious people always have. They cannot be indifferent to human well-being, because they have arranged the cosmos with a view to its order, and it would be out of character for them to be unconcerned about the possibility of order in human life. All the material resources that come to us through the motion of the sun and the other spheres are an expression of divine concern for human life. The controlling motions of nature are rightly honoured and worshipped, then, because nature is shot through with an order that derives from beings of the greatest intelligence and virtue. And since we too have souls, we are made of such stuff as are these divine governors. We share a 'common origin' with the gods, as the Athenian says to the young man in the passage cited above. He also holds that we should express our appreciation for the gods by taking them as models for the way we live, and we do this best by sharing in the governance of the polis. The gods continually attend to the common good of the cosmos, and so we too should be public-spirited contributors to the good of our local community.

Magnesia might be called a theocracy – a city ruled by god – because its founders (the Athenian and his two interlocutors) are convinced that divine beings govern human life and that publicly organized religious rituals must acknowledge their sovereignty over us. The Greek word for 'god' (*theos*) is the first word of the *Laws*, and one of the major themes of the work is our indebtedness to divine oversight. But above all Magnesia is a city that is governed by human reason. Its rulers are not priests, and it is not organized around a sacrosanct text of unquestionable authority.

The *Laws* nominates itself as required reading for all Magnesians; it is the book around which civic life is to be organized. But its claim to authority rests on reason: every institution it prescribes is to be accepted not because divine will so wishes it but because philosophical arguments support those social arrangements. We should remind ourselves that the *Laws* is meant to be part of a more comprehensive philosophical framework, in that it builds on the fundamental premise of the *Republic* that social unity is the pre-eminent good of human life – a premise that in turn rests on Plato's hypothesis that measure and due proportion are precisely what goodness is. When the Athenian says to the young man that 'what is best for you to do for the universe turns out to be best for you as well', he is drawing upon the thesis, established by Socrates in the *Republic*, that when one does one's proper part in just social arrangements, one is promoting not only the well-being of others, but one's own as well.

We should not suppose, then, that in the *Laws* Plato has lost his confidence in the power of human reason to find its way, and has therefore turned to something else – faith, authority, tradition – to take its place. On the contrary, the essential ideas of the *Euthyphro* are still in place in the *Laws*. Socrates insists in that early work that piety is not constituted by whatever it is that the gods favour. Rather, the gods themselves are constrained in their attitudes by their perception of what piety is. When they approve of some person or action, that is because they realize that it possesses a property that justifies their favour. Similarly, the *Laws* conceives of divine beings as rational agents who have constructed the cosmos for a reason – that is, because it is good that it be so constructed. They look to the good to determine what to do; all the more reason why we should do the same. Our goal must be to act for the sake of the good of the whole, not to do whatever it is that is pleasing to the gods.

Nonetheless, there is one way in which religion plays a far

larger role in the *Laws* than in the *Republic*. In the *Republic* Socrates insists that we leave aside all thought of divine rewards and punishments when we inquire into the reasons for being a just person. The argument that justice is a virtue of extraordinary value to the just person is entirely independent of the existence of gods who care about human life, and so it should have as much force for an atheist as for a religious believer. Someone who accepts the principal thesis of the *Republic* – that justice is a great good – would be an outstanding citizen of any city, and there would be no need for the city in which he lives to take special measures, as Magnesia does, to ensure that he recognize the existence of divine providence. Why then has Plato written a dialogue in which the main interlocutor insists that if citizens publicly question the existence of gods or their interest in human well-being, civil authorities must try to show them that they are mistaken, and if they cannot be persuaded, they must be punished with death? The Athenian fears the consequences of widespread atheism, but he should not fear that citizens will become unjust people simply because they hold that there are no gods or that they are indifferent to us. They need only be given a copy of the *Republic*, and, having become convinced that justice is a great good, they will never willingly do what is unjust. Why then should it matter whether they are atheists or not?

Plato presumably recognizes that it is unrealistic to expect a whole political community to follow the complex argument of the *Republic* and be brought to see the great intrinsic value of being just. Socrates, as depicted in the early dialogues, has only limited success with his interlocutors. Perhaps for this reason Plato is convinced that ordinary citizens will for the most part resist the thesis of the *Republic* that justice and other virtues are inherently good and therefore do not require a grounding in religion. Some people do not need any sort of argument for being just; they are by disposition cooperative and naturally love justice and hate injustice. If such decent people also happened to be atheists, their atheism would not detract in the least from their disposition to be good citizens. But this natural love of justice is unusual, and there are forces at work in most people that will deflect them from doing what social justice requires, unless those forces are outmatched by countervailing influences. Most people care a great deal – more than they should – about what is good for them and for their families and friends. Because it leaves the traditional household intact, Magnesia leaves in place psychological tendencies that threaten to undermine the commitment of citizens to the good of the whole community.

To convince citizens to devote themselves to the public good, the Athenian points to socially salutary truths about the governance of the cosmos that ordinary people can easily come to recognize, because they are very close to what people have always believed. That Zeus and the other gods who govern the natural world care about justice among human beings was a commonplace of Plato's time, and was endorsed by many poets. Those traditional ideas, the Athenian supposes, can be demonstrated to anyone who has an open mind. Real divinities can be shown to be outstandingly intelligent and virtuous, and to govern our lives to the best of their ability. They would never let injustice go unpunished, or justice unrewarded. Arguments for these facts about the gods are within the reach of ordinary people – far more so than the arguments of Plato's dialogues for the existence of forms and the nature of justice.

The argument of the *Laws* that leads to the conclusion that we are the beneficiaries of divine providence is Plato's own cosmology, but he believes that this component of his philosophy can become the basis of a public religion that supports a well-governed political community. Widespread atheism, he fears, would undermine social justice, and no lies need be told to combat it. Most people would like to see themselves as a portion of a larger order – an order that spans over great regions of time and space, and connects our brief lives with an unending whole and an all-encompassing intelligence. Plato has no quarrel with that human inclination. He thinks he sees how it can be satisfied in a way that makes no appeal to comforting falsehoods. He is not innovating, when he conceives of his second-best political community as one that is shot through with public religious practices. What is most noteworthy about the public religion of Magnesia is that it has its roots not in tradition, convention, or authority, but in philosophical reasons – reasons that can be given to anyone who has an open mind and enough intelligence to understand them. The ultimate source of political authority, in Magnesia no less than in Kallipolis, is the power of the human mind to understand what is good.

Plato's thoughts about religion, morality and politics are so rich and fruitful that they have been appropriated by many later philosophical traditions. To Christian thinkers he provides arguments for the immortality of the soul, the existence of a divine and caring creator, and the supreme importance of the moral life. But when the authors of the Greek and Roman worlds became more widely available to European philosophers of the modern age, Plato's dialogues also provided material for challenging traditional Christian doctrine. The supreme entity of Platonic philosophy is the form of the good, not a divine person. He acknowledges that an atheist can be no less devoted to justice and other moral values than a theist. Nothing in his philosophy corresponds to the Christian notion of faith. Every human institution must be based on reason. We are to abide by principles of justice and serve our community not because a divine being commands us to do so or will reward us if we are compliant, but because philosophical reasoning shows how great a good justice is. Reason can reshape our world and the forms should guide that project, but we must be realistic about how strong the forces of unreason are. They dwell within the souls of each of us, and create corrupt societies dominated by the love of wealth, power and luxury. Few people will ever have the talent and good fortune to master the inner beasts that disfigure human beings and make them unhappy. Socrates was one of them. Plato's dialogues were written to inspire and educate more.

CHRONOLOGY

***c*.485 BC** Birth of Protagoras, prominent sophist, in Abdera (northern Greece).

***c*.485 BC** Birth of Gorgias, prominent teacher of rhetoric, in Leontini (Sicily).

469 BC Birth of Socrates in Athens.

460 BC Birth of Democritus, founder of atomism, in Abdera.

460–450 BC Aristophanes, comic dramatist, born in Athens some time in this decade.

443 BC Protagoras writes the legal code for Thurii, a Greek colony.

431 BC Outbreak of Peloponnesian War between Sparta and Athens, recounted by Thucydides.

***c*.430 BC** Birth of Xenophon, Athenian general and author of a book of reminiscences of Socrates, in Athens.

427 BC Birth of Plato in Athens.

423 BC Aristophanes's *Clouds*, ridiculing Socrates, produced in Athens.

***c*.415 BC** Protagoras dies.

404 BC Peloponnesian War ends with the defeat of Athens by Sparta. Athenian democracy overthrown. Rule of the Thirty.

403 BC Defeat of the Thirty and restoration of democracy in Athens.

399 BC Trial and death of Socrates. Gorgias dies several years later.

388 BC Plato visits Pythagorean mathematicians in Sicily.

387 BC Plato founds the Academy, which remains in existence through the first century BG.

386 BC Death of Aristophanes.

384 BC Birth of Aristotle in Stagira (northern Greece).

367 BC Aristotle arrives in Athens to study with members of Plato's Academy.

367 BC Plato returns to Sicily to guide the regime of Dionysius II.

361 BC Plato again travels to Sicily to influence its politics.

347 BC Death of Plato. Aristotle departs from Athens.

341 BC Birth of Epicurus, founder of hedonistic school, in Samos (island close to the coast of modern Turkey).

335 BC Aristotle returns to Athens and founds his own school, the Lyceum.

322 BC Death of Aristotle.

***c*.307 BC** Epicurus establishes his school in Athens.

300 BC Zeno of Citium establishes the Stoic school in Athens.

SUGGESTIONS FOR FURTHER READING

The best collection of Plato's writings translated into English is *Plato: Complete Works*, edited by John M. Cooper (Hackett Publishing Co., 1997). Hackett and Oxford University Press have also published translations of individual dialogues, and these are generally of high quality. The Loeb Classical Library, published by Harvard University Press, contains translations of the dialogues with Greek and English on facing pages. R. E. Allen has translated many of the dialogues with commentary for Yale University Press. Several of the dialogues appear with extensive commentary in the Clarendon Plato Series published by the Clarendon Press. Other noteworthy translations of individual works are: *Republic*, translated by Tom Griffith (Cambridge University Press, 2000); *Republic*, translated by C. D. C. Reeve (Hackett Publishing Co., 2004); and *Laws*, translated by Thomas L. Pangle (Basic Books, 1980).

Debra Nails, *The People of Plato* (Hackett, 2002), provides information about the individuals who speak or are referred to in Plato's works. On the political climate of fifth- and fourth-century BC Athens, see two works by Josiah Ober: *Mass and Elite in Democratic Athens* (Princeton University Press, 1989) and *Political Dissent in Democratic Athens* (Princeton University Press, 1998). Other treatments of Plato's intellectual and political milieu are: Peter Krentz, *The Thirty at Athens* (Cornell University Press, 1982); and George Kerferd, *The Sophistic Movement* (Cambridge University Press, 1981). The political writings of the sophists can be found in Michael Gagarin and Paul Woodruff (eds.), *Early*

Greek Political Thought from Homer to the Sophists (Cambridge University Press, 1995). On Democritus and other presocratic thinkers, see W. K. C. Guthrie, *A History of Greek Philosophy*, vols. 1 and 2 (Cambridge University Press, 1962 and 1965); and G. S. Kirk, J. E. Raven, and M. Schofield, *The Presocratic Philosophers* (2nd ed., Cambridge University Press, 1983).

For collections of essays on all aspects of Plato's philosophy, see Richard Kraut (ed.), *The Cambridge Companion to Plato* (Cambridge University Press, 1992); Gail Fine (ed.), *Plato*, 2 volumes (Oxford University Press, 1999); Gail Fine (ed.), *The Oxford Handbook of Plato* (Oxford University Press, 2008); and the 'Plato' entry of the online *Stanford Encyclopedia of Philosophy* (http://plato.stanford.edu/).

On the early dialogues, see Thomas C. Brickhouse and Nicholas D. Smith, *The Philosophy of Socrates* (Westview Press, 2000); Charles H. Kahn, *Plato and the Socratic Dialogue* (Cambridge University Press, 1996); Mark McPherran, *The Religion of Socrates* (Pennsylvania State Press, 1996); and Gregory Vlastos, *Socrates: Ironist and Moral Philosopher* (Cambridge University Press, 1991). Vlastos's book is an important attempt to distinguish the philosophies of Socrates and Plato and to view the early dialogues as the record of Plato's gradual philosophical development. For scepticism about such an approach, see Debra Nails, *Agora, Academy, and the Conduct of Philosophy* (Kluwer Academic Publishers, 1995). For a collection of essays on central Socratic doctrines and his influence on later philosophical traditions, see Sara Ahbel-Rappe and Rachana Kamtekar, *A Companion to Socrates* (Blackwell Publishing, 2006).

For studies of individual early works, see C. D. C. Reeve, *Socrates in the Apology* (Hackett Publishing Co., 1989); Dominic Scott, *Plato's Meno* (Cambridge University Press, 2006); and Terry Penner and Christopher Rowe, *Plato's Lysis* (Cambridge University Press, 2005). Richard Kraut, *Socrates and the State* (Princeton University Press, 1984), is a study of the *Crito* and the political orientation of the early dialogues.

Ruby Blondell's *The Play of Character in Plato's Dialogues* (Cambridge University Press, 2002) emphasizes the dramatic aspect of Plato's writing, with close attention to his portrayal of his interlocutors. It applies this method of reading to the *Hippias Minor, Republic, Theaetetus, Sophist* and *Statesman*.

Discussions of Plato's metaphysics and epistemology can be found in Allan Silverman, *The Dialectic of Essence: A Study of Plato's Metaphysics* (Princeton University Press, 2002); Mary Margaret McCabe, *Plato's Individuals* (Princeton University Press, 1994); Nicholas P. White, *Plato on Knowledge and Reality* (Hackett Publishing Co., 1976); Terry Penner, *The Ascent from Nominalism* (D. Reidel Publishing Company, 1987); and R. M. Dancy, *Plato's Introduction of Forms* (Cambridge University Press, 2004).

On Plato's moral philosophy, see Terence Irwin, *Plato's Ethics* (Oxford University Press, 1995). A treatment of his political philosophy, portraying the *Laws* as a turn away from the authoritarianism of the *Republic*, is provided by Christopher Bobonich, *Plato's Utopia Recast* (Oxford University Press, 2002). For a study of the *Laws*, see Glenn R. Morrow, *Plato's Cretan City* (Princeton University Press, 1960). S. Sara Monoson, *Plato's Democratic Entanglements* (Princeton University Press, 2000), shows the influence of Athenian institutions and culture on Plato's political thinking.

On the *Republic*, consult Julia Annas, *An Introduction to Plato's Republic* (Oxford University Press, 1981); G. R. F. Ferrari (ed.), *The Cambridge Companion to Plato's Republic* (Cambridge University Press, 2007); Richard Kraut (ed.), *Critical Essays on Plato's Republic* (Rowman & Littlefield, 1997); C. D. C. Reeve, *Philosopher-Kings* (Princeton University Press, 1988); and Gerasimos Santas (ed.), *The Blackwell Guide to Plato's Republic* (Blackwell, 2006).

On the *Symposium*, see Frisbee C. C. Sheffield, *Plato's Symposium* (Oxford University Press, 2006), and J. H. Lesher, Debra Nails, and Frisbee C. C. Sheffield (eds.), *Plato's Symposium* (Center for Hellenic Studies, 2006).

To study Plato's refutation of Protagorean relativism, one should consult two guides to the *Theaetetus*: Myles Burnyeat, *The Theaetetus of Plato* (Hackett Publishing Co., 1990), and D. N. Sedley, *The Midwife of Platonism* (Clarendon Press, 2004).

For help with some of Plato's difficult late dialogues, see T. K. Johansen, *Plato's Natural Philosophy* (Cambridge University Press, 2004); M. S. Lane, *Method and Politics in Plato's Statesman* (Cambridge University Press, 1998); and Constance C. Meinwald, *Plato's Parmenides* (Oxford University Press, 1991).

On Plato's influence on nineteenth- and twentieth-century philosophers, see M. S. Lane, *Plato's Modern Progeny* (Duckworth, 2001); and Catherine H. Zuckert, *Postmodern Platos* (University of Chicago Press, 1996).

INDEX